➡ DEDICATION

From Julia

For Patty Hearst, Rosie Ruiz, Anne Heche, Whitney Houston, Amy Fisher, Martha Stewart, Sarah Palin, Lindsay Lohan, Ms. Teen South Carolina, Eve, and every inspired woman who ever reached for it (really, really reached for it) and dreamed big.

From Lou

This book is humbly dedicated to Andrea Muirragui Davis, a friend, co-worker, damn fierce poker player, and fighter.

➡ TABLE OF CONTENTS

INTRODUCTION 8
HOW TO USE THIS BOOK 10
HOW NOT TO USE THIS BOOK 12

PART 1: EXCUSES BY SITUATION 14
Excuses for BAD HABITS 16
Excuses for a BAD HAIR DAY 22
Excuses for BAD HOUSEKEEPING 28
Excuses for BAD JUDGMENT 34
Excuses for BEING THE OTHER WOMAN 40
Excuses for BEING PASSED OVER FOR A JOB 46
Excuses for DISAPPOINTING YOUR BOOK CLUB 52
Excuses for BREAKING UP 56
Excuses for COMPROMISING PHOTOS 64
Excuses for COMPROMISING YOUR DREAMS 70
Excuses for COOKING (NOT) 74
Excuses for BEING A CRAZY EX-GIRLFRIEND 80
Excuses for THE DAY AFTER 86
Excuses for DOING A DRIVE-BY 90
Excuses for FASHION MISTAKES 94
Excuses for GIVING AWAY A SECRET 100
Excuses for PLAYING THE GRANDMOTHER CARD 104
Excuses for LATENESS/NOT SHOWING UP 108
Excuses for LAZINESS/GENERAL SLOTH 112

Excuses for MISSING A PERIOD 116

Excuses for BEING THE MOM 120

Excuses for PIGGING OUT 126

Excuses for SHOPPING 132

Excuses for SISTER RIVALRY 138

Excuses for SMOKING 142

Excuses for BAD STUDY HABITS 146

Excuses for TATTOOS 150

Excuses for OFFICE DRAMA 154

Excuses for PURSE MALFUNCTION 158

The Ultimate Excuse: PMS 162

PART 2: REAL AND IMAGINARY GREAT WOMEN'S EXCUSES 164

Excuses for EVE 166

Excuses for GREAT WOMEN OF FICTION 167

Excuses for JOCASTA 167

Excuses for JULIET 168

Excuses for MADAME BOVARY 169

Excuses for CINDERELLA 170

Excuses for THE OLD WOMAN WHO LIVED IN A SHOE 170

Excuses for RAPUNZEL 171

Excuses for SLEEPING BEAUTY.....................................171

Excuses for SNOW WHITE 172

Excuses for LADY CHATTERLEY.....................................172

Excuses for MRS. VOORHEES 173

Excuses for THE WOMEN OF "SEX AND THE CITY".............174

Excuses for THE WICKED WITCH OF THE WEST 175

PART 3: EXCUSES FOR GREAT WOMEN IN HISTORY 176
Excuses for DELILAH 177
Excuses for JEZEBEL 178
Excuses for SALOME 179
Excuses for MARY 180
Excuses for CLEOPATRA 180
Excuses for JOAN OF ARC 181
Excuses for LUCREZIA BORGIA 181
Excuses for LADY GODIVA 182
Excuses for BETSY ROSS 183
Excuses for MARIE-ANTOINETTE......................................184
Excuses for FLORENCE NIGHTINGALE 185
Excuses for ROSIE THE RIVETER 186
Excuses for HELEN KELLER 186
Excuses for LIZZIE BORDEN 187
Excuses for EVA PERON 188
Excuses for BONNIE PARKER 189
Excuses for TYPHOID MARY 189
Excuses for TOKYO ROSE 190
Excuses for AMELIA EARHART 190
Excuses for JUDY GARLAND 191
Excuses for JOAN CRAWFORD 192
Excuses for ELIZABETH TAYLOR 193
Excuses for MARILYN MONROE 194
Excuses for ROSA PARKS 195
Excuses for CHER 195
Excuses for OPRAH WINFREY 196

Excuses for **MADONNA** 196
Excuses for **TONYA HARDING** 197
Excuses for **LINDSAY LOHAN, PARIS HILTON, ET AL.** 198
Excuses for **HILLARY RODHAM CLINTON** 199

INDEX OF EXCUSES 200
ABOUT THE AUTHORS 208

INTRODUCTION

It's not our fault. It's your fault, really. Okay, maybe not you personally, but you the book buyer. The literary enthusiast.

Your fondness for and interest in our previous book, *The Complete Excuses Handbook: The Definitive Guide to Avoiding Blame and Shirking Responsibility for All Your Own Miserable Failings and Sloppy Mistakes*, led us to believe that there might be interest in a similar treatise, but one focused on issues directly related to women. It's not like women can't have their own spinoffs, you know. Ever heard of a little thing called the WNBA? No? Well, never mind then.

Of course, you may not actually be aware of that other book either, in which case you may be wondering: a.) why we are blaming you for *The Complete Excuses Handbook: Women's Edition*; and/or b.) whether or not you need to read the first book before diving into this one.

Well, a., we aren't blaming you. So relax. Don't get your Spanks in a bunch. Let's not start off on the wrong foot here. And b., no, you don't need to read the previous book first, but we're not going to put up a fight if you decide you'd like to.

All of this, of course, is kind of beside the point. The point of an introduction is to introduce, so here we go.

Julia and Lou, your fearless guides through this rocky terrain of apologies, pleas, and tamperings of the truth, would like to welcome you to *The Complete Excuses Handbook: Women's Edition*. Both writers have a long and shameless history of thinking on their feet, and they share with you their expertise in the fine art of coming up with excuses in almost every imaginable scenario. As you will soon find out, some have met with success, and some have not. Take the wisdom offered on these pages, and do with it what you wish.

And, um, don't blame them if things kind of blow up in your face. This whole thing was your fault anyway. Remember?

How to
USE THIS BOOK

We realize that some men, out of curiosity or for educational value, will be reading these words (one is, in fact, helping to write them). But, like movies on Lifetime, we aren't going to address that audience. We are going to be talking directly to women, making the assumption that you, the reader, are female.

And, unlike a male, you are not afraid of reading directions. Which is why you are here on the "How to Use This Book" page and not galumphing ahead without guidance.

The directions are simple. To use this book effectively, you can take one of three approaches:

1. Browse randomly for ideas. This may, at first, seem similar to the male galumphing approach, but it's really more purposeful and less awkward. It's jumping around with a rationale and philosophy rather than jumping around because your DNA doesn't allow you to do much else.

2. You could use the book the old-fashioned way by starting your journey with the Table of Contents, which is arranged by situation. Need an excuse involving a relationship issue? You can go right to the sections labeled "Excuses for Lateness/Not Showing Up," "Excuses for Breaking Up," "Excuses for The Day After," "Excuses for Being a Crazy Ex-Girlfriend," or "Excuses for Doing a Drive-by" and have your needs immediately met.

3. Your third choice is to start at the end, using the index as your guide to finding the pros and cons of specific excuses.

The choice is yours.

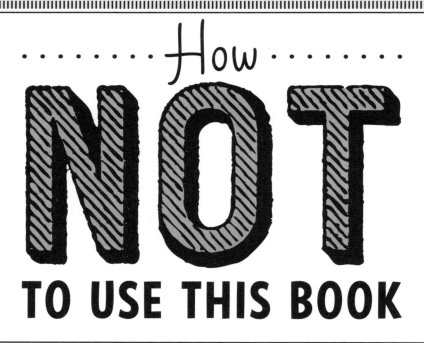

How NOT TO USE THIS BOOK

- → As something to hurl at another human being who doesn't buy your excuse.
- → As an excuse for not reading your book club selection.
- → As part of a smoke-and-purification ritual.
- → As a hammer.
- → As a disclaimer in a court of law.

·········· part 1 ··········
EXCUSES
by SITUATION

EXCUSES FOR
BAD HABITS

Bad habits are the ideal breeding ground for excuses. After all, when you call something a habit, you are admitting that you don't necessarily do it for pleasure or any other positive consequence. You are doing it without thinking. So, sue you.

All of this makes coming up with an excuse for a bad habit even more awkward. Even though you may not think about your habit, you do have to think about what you are going to say when it needs rationalizing.

➡ IT'S SOMETHING I STARTED IN COLLEGE

Nice try. And you might get away with it if graduation was just a year or so in your past. But if you've stored this one away in your hope chest and pulled it out while playing mahjong at the senior citizen's center, don't expect much sympathy.

➡ I DON'T DO IT ALL THE TIME

But the fact that you are doing it now is clearly causing issues.

➡ I ONLY DO IT WHEN I DRINK

Of course, you only do it when you drink. Of course. Now, let me just hold your hair while you lean over the toilet. After you brush your teeth, you can tell me all about how you only do this when you drink.

➡ YOU'RE THE ONLY PERSON WHO KNOWS

There's a definite pleasure in being the only person who knows a deep secret or embarrassing detail about someone's life. So, out of sheer flattery, you might be buying some time when you whisper this little pearl into somebody's ear.

Soon, though, your confidante will begin to wonder what other secrets you've been keeping, how many other people you've told this one to—and how many secrets you've been telling people about her.

➡ I'M AN ADULT

Yes, you are. Which doesn't explain why you are acting like a four-year-old.

➡ [Insert accomplished person's name here] DID IT, TOO

Sure. Fine. There's precedent. But remember back in third grade when you tried to pull the "He did it, too" excuse? Did it work for you then? Well, guess what? It's likely to be just as effective now.

➡ PLEASE DON'T JUDGE ME

This approach has the benefit of making the person you say it to feel like the bad guy. It shifts attention away from your own unpleasant behavior and onto the psychological fragility of another. After all, people can be so judgmental. And clearly, you are the victim here.

➡ I'M TRYING TO QUIT

"Let's look forward—into the near or distant future—and not at the unflattering image directly in front of us," is what you are suggesting when you trot out this excuse, which is actually more of a diversion than an outright plea. If nothing else, it will briefly delay your accountability.

➡ IT'S NOT LIKE I'M PROUD OF THIS

Conveying a sense of your own disgust at what you are doing does have a certain cache. It shows that you have depth and a fully functioning conscience. There is also a tinge of angst, which people tend to eat up.

➡ I AM A PRODUCT OF MY ENVIRONMENT

If you can put this much thought into the sociological impact of your past, surely you can figure out a way to stop picking at your cuticles.

ADDITIONAL EXCUSES FOR
BAD HABITS

➤ I'M PART OF A MAJOR SCIENTIFIC EXPERIMENT THAT I'M CONTRACTUALLY OBLIGATED NOT TO TALK ABOUT. I SHOULDN'T EVEN BE TELLING YOU WHAT I'VE ALREADY SAID. THIS CONVERSATION NEVER OCCURRED.

➤ THE DEAL ON MY NEW REALITY SHOW SAYS THAT I CAN'T EXPLAIN MYSELF UNTIL THE SHOW LAUNCHES ON FOX.

➤ IT'S MEDICINAL. SERIOUSLY, DUDE. I'VE GOT THAT EYE THING.

➤ THAT LONG, DECORATIVE GLASS TUBE OVER THERE BY THE BAG OF DORITOS? IT'S A VASE.

➤ **WHAT DO YOU HAVE AGAINST MY HABIT? NUNS HAVE WORN HABITS FOR CENTURIES. JUST BECAUSE MINE IS A LITTLE SHABBY, DOESN'T MEAN YOU SHOULD BE SO RUDE AS TO CALL IT A "BAD HABIT." THE NERVE.**

➤ **MY DOCTOR SAID IT'S NOT HEALTHY TO HOLD IT IN.**

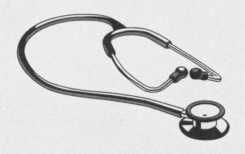

EXCUSES FOR A BAD HAIR DAY

Sometimes the hair gods leave you hanging. Despite your best efforts, curls get kinky; precision cuts take on mullet traits; and cowlicks defy both gravity and the round brush. But sometimes, on those days when (admit it) you hit the snooze button a few too many times to give your tresses proper attention, you need to get creative with more than just a flatiron.

⇒ I WENT TO BED WITH WET HAIR

Especially convincing when accompanied by a nasty looking rat's nest at the back of the head or random patches of flatness at the temples, this approach even has a noble air of girl scout preparedness. People might be impressed by your preemptive grooming, all the better to hit the morning running. Best not to mention that the reason you opted for an evening shower over a morning one was because you had to wash the bar smell out of your hair before turning in at 3 a.m.

⇒ I TRIED SOME NEW PRODUCT

Who hasn't been lured by a label's claim to turn flat hair into a full, luxurious pouf or to condition some sense into unruly locks? It gives us hope. When the newest and most promising potion turns out to be nothing more than a recipe for an oil-slicked mane—or worse—you can expect some sympathetic (better-you-than-me-sister) nods from onlookers. This excuse also works when you simply didn't bother to wash out yesterday's product.

⇒ I'M GROWING IT OUT

Like so many things in life, hair struggles with transition. It isn't a pretty phase, and it can drag on for months—which is about how long it takes for this excuse to reach its expiration date. Unless you are joining a cult or going for a Guinness record, there will come a day when people will look at your barrettes and headbands and think, "That woman has given up."

➤ I CAN'T DO BANGS

Problem is, it's hard to take somebody seriously when she looks a little like cousin Oliver from The Brady Bunch.

➤ I'M PARTING IT DIFFERENTLY

Changing the topography of your head will throw people off enough that they might not notice a multitude of other sins, like dark roots, too much mousse, or the telltale ridges of hat head. Let them be distracted by the change, but keep in mind that the magic here is novelty. (Then again, once the novelty wears off, you can always go back to your original part . . . rinse, and repeat.)

➤ I HAVE SUCH FINE HAIR

Super-fine hair is a curse worthy of its own telethon. It has fueled the business of hair extensions, volumizing sprays, FDA testing, and hair-style magazines chock-full of chops, bobs, and lightly layered mid-length 'dos. It also makes a darned handy excuse when it is clear that you've rejected all of the above for the classic ponytail copout.

➤ MY ELECTRICITY WENT OUT THIS MORNING

Ted Kaczynski never used that excuse. And just look at the fabulous head of hair on that guy.

➡ I TOLD MY HAIRDRESSER I WANTED TO TRY SOMETHING DIFFERENT

While it's easy to blame an abomination on someone who has access to auburn hair dye and number 4 gauge clippers, this approach will not get you off scot-free. The fact is, you were complicit in the crime, and your Flock of Seagulls comb-over can't hide the guilt in your eyes.

➡ I'M BETWEEN HAIRDRESSERS

Last time we checked, they weren't giving out medals for being non-committal. Those feathered bangs don't make you look any prettier sitting on the fence.

➡ I JUST WANTED IT OUT OF MY EYES

Those words sound innocent enough. But let's not forget that the desire to pull hair off one's forehead brought us two of the most regrettable accessories in history: the banana clip and the scrunchie. Groom responsibly, ladies.

➡ IT LOOKED CUTE ON RENEE ZELLWEGER

And you, my friend, are not Renee Zellweger.

➡ IT'S A NEW PERM

Lucky for you, the sun will come out . . . tomorrow.

➡ THE BOX SAID IT WAS TEMPORARY COLOR

This excuse comes with a hint of comic relief, as the person doling it out is often wide-eyed beneath a shock of chartreuse or midnight blue. If only out of pity, people will take you seriously when you plead misleading packaging—after they catch their breath from laughing hysterically.

ADDITIONAL EXCUSES FOR A
BAD HAIR DAY

➤➤ FOR ME, THIS IS A GOOD HAIR DAY.

➤➤ MEN LOVE THE THE THREE STOOGES, RIGHT?
THIS IS THE LARRY LOOK.

➤➤ MY FOLLICLES EXPLODED.

➤➤ NEW PILLOWS.

➤➤ THIS IS MY NATURAL HAIR COLOR.
I JUST DYE THE ROOTS DARK.

➤➤ THEY CALL THIS THE 'JUST ROLLED OUT OF
BED' LOOK.

➤➤ THE BOWL SLIPPED.

EXCUSES FOR BAD HOUSEKEEPING

Remember that moment when you first walked into what would become your home or apartment? Remember that sense of everything having a place? Remember the shine of the floors and the smell of unsullied carpet?

Now, remember a week later. Remember the careless spill? Remember the drawer that was supposed to be just for dish towels but that now houses batteries, a lint brush, your matchbook collection, an orphaned hot roller, some knee highs, a calculator (when did you get a calculator?), and some unidentified phone number scribbled on a cocktail napkin?

Remember a month later, when you found yourself picking outfits directly from the laundry piled in the living room? Or the next month, when you gave up even getting the laundry out of the dryer before putting the items back into rotation?

Remember the home-cooked meals you thought you were going to make? And that "I'll-get-it-later" moment when the box of macaroni dumped between the stove and the counter?

Well, we feel your pain. Housekeeping excuses are used not only to placate friends and family who cast their gazes around your abode with that terrified look in their eyes, but also to placate ourselves.

➤ I RAN OUT OF SWIFFERS

One of the beauties of using a specific cleaning system (as opposed to the standard broom and vacuum cleaner) is that they come in a finite supply and therefore carry a built-in excuse for eventually living in your own filth. Whenever you run the risk of being a dust-bunny breeder, just lay the blame on the missing part.

➤ THOSE DIRTY DISHES AREN'T GOING ANYWHERE

Well, they aren't going anywhere right now. But give them time. In a few days, they stand a chance of getting carried away by an army of ravenous insects.

➤ IT'S NOT MY WEEKEND TO CLEAN

Having roommates or a domestic partner gives you—as long as they aren't within earshot—an ideal scapegoat for all things dirty and unkempt. Just don't try the same excuse two weekends in a row.

➤ I'M NOT YOUR MAID

This is a good excuse to throw at others in your household when expectations continually shift to you to keep up appearances. Of course, those people aren't exactly dressed in tiny black skirts with white aprons, either. So be careful how bluntly and how often you use this one.

➡ I'M NOT YOUR MOTHER

Try to refrain from using this if you are, in fact, their mother.

➡ IT'S SO HARD TO GET KIDS TO DO THEIR CHORES

What friend doesn't understand how lazy these kids today are, what with their text messaging and their facebooking and their pinball machines, and whatnot that keep them from fulfilling their household obligations? Of course, blaming the kids doesn't speak very well of your skills at enforcing the clean-up rules. And, of course, the excuse runs out of steam once they've left the nest.

➡ MY CLEANING WOMAN QUIT

Inside, the person hearing this excuse might be thinking, "Yeah, I'd quit, too, if I had to deal with a dump like this." Plus, you lose any chance of garnering the sympathy vote for sounding a little too much like Imelda Marcos.

➡ IT HAS SENTIMENTAL VALUE

Nobody (except maybe your mother) expects your digs to look like a model apartment. But when the living room begins to look like a branch of the Ripley's Believe It or Not Museum, it's time to introduce yourself to the attic or storage unit and their possible uses.

➡ I'M IN THE PROCESS OF DECLUTTERING

On the positive side, this excuse makes it sound as if you are actually working on the problem. On the negative side, it leads the listener to wonder how bad the place could possibly have been before you started getting down to business.

➡ I'M DEFROSTING NEXT WEEK

Will it take that long for Admiral Perry to organize the expedition?

➡ EINSTEIN HAD A CLUTTERED HOUSE

So do crazy cat ladies.

ADDITIONAL EXCUSES FOR
BAD HOUSEKEEPING

➤ MICE NEED A SAFE PLACE TO LIVE, TOO.
THIS MESSAGE BROUGHT TO YOU BY PETA.

➤ THE HOUSE REQUIRES LESS HEATING THIS WAY.

➤ I HAVE A BOOK THAT SAYS THAT AN ORGANIZED
HOUSE IS A STERILE, UNCREATIVE HOUSE. I'D
SHOW YOU THE BOOK, BUT I CAN'T SEEM TO
FIND IT.

➤ CLEANING GIVES ME CARPAL TUNNEL
SYNDROME.

➤ NATURE ABHORS A VACUUM.

➤ I AM MAKING MY OWN PENICILLIN.

➤ MY ARMS DON'T BEND THAT WAY.

➤ YOU MEAN THIS ISN'T WHAT THEY MEAN BY
ELBOW GREASE?

EXCUSES FOR BAD JUDGMENT

Sometimes it's obvious right after you make a decision. Sometimes bad judgment doesn't become evident until long after the damage has been done and the consequences wrest control and take the upper hand.

Whether it's at one of those extremes or anywhere in between, your bad judgment needs an exit strategy. Or, at least, a way to mitigate. Here are some that might do the job:

➡ I HAD A LITTLE TOO MUCH TO DRINK

We all know that the fiction in that sentence is "a little." It's not "a little" that takes you over the line. It's "a lot." But saying "I had a lot too much to drink" could get you in even more trouble. Plus, it's bad grammar.

➡ SINCE WHEN IS THAT ILLEGAL?

Ignorance may be bliss, but it won't get you out of having to do some serious clean-up after a major infraction. Try this one if you must. Just not with a cop.

➡ WE RECONNECTED ON FACEBOOK

Ah, Facebook, the website that has connected everyone to everyone—including old friends from high school, college, and other past lives who might have been better left in the past. Even connections that start with some pleasant reminiscences about the good old days can degenerate into major awkwardness—like a John Hughes movie in reverse. And once the reunion exits the Internet and is sitting there across the table from you at a coffeehouse, making up for lost time in the "let me tell you how much my life sucks" department, there is no real-life button you can click for Unfriending.

Some things are best left at the keyboard.

➡ HE WAS REALLY HOT IN HIGH SCHOOL

A nice companion to the Facebook explanation, this more focused version carries with it your own mistaken assumption that things stay the same and that there is no such thing as male-patterned baldness.

➡ I DIDN'T KNOW HE HAD A GIRLFRIEND/WIFE

At some point in the very beginning, you might not have known about the girlfriend/wife. Apparently, it didn't come up in the conversation. But did you ask? And did there come a point (like the time you wanted to write down his address and he gave you a p.o. box . . . or the time he checked into the hotel room under an alias . . . or the time you found the drawer in his bathroom full of cosmetics that were not yours) when you wondered if something might be up?

And what happened then? See also: Excuses for Being the Other Woman.

➡ I ALWAYS GO FOR THE BAD BOY

And doesn't that explain why you always end up crying in your room over a quart of Häagan Dazs?

➡ HE'S A DIAMOND IN THE ROUGH

This line of thinking may have worked for Adalaide in *Guys and Dolls* (although the curtain went down at their wedding, so we don't really know), but it probably isn't going to work for you.

Keep in mind that it takes millions of years and very specific conditions for a lump of coal to become a diamond. Do you really have that kind of time?

ADDITIONAL EXCUSES FOR
BAD JUDGEMENT

➤ HE LOOKED REALLY CUTE ON HIS WANTED POSTER.

➤ HE WON ME IN A DRAG RACE. I HAD NO CHOICE.

➤ I WASN'T WEARING MY GLASSES WHEN WE MET.

➤ IT'S THE DRUGS TALKING.

➤ **CLOTHES MAKE ME LOOK FAT.**

➤ **I DECIDED TO SLEEP ON IT. I MEAN HIM.**

➤ **I GET MIGRAINES WHEN I THINK THINGS THROUGH.**

➤ **COWBOYS ARE MY WEAKNESS. AND FIREMEN.**

EXCUSES FOR BEING THE
OTHER WOMAN

At the moment when you find out for yourself that you are, in fact, the third angle in a triangle, you are likely to garner enormous sympathy. Imagine the shock. Imagine the sense of betrayal. Imagine the outrage that you experience when discovering that your partner has a very significant other. At that particular moment, sympathy is on your side.

Now flash forward to a moment six months after you discover that you are the other woman—and you are still the other woman. Here, you are likely to find significantly fewer shoulders to cry on. Ponder these excuses:

➡ HE'S GOING THROUGH A ROUGH TIME IN HIS MARRIAGE

Maybe he is. But last time we checked, the vows weren't "'Til rough times do us get a little tired of each other."

➡ HE'S GOING THROUGH A SEPARATION

A step above "He's going through a rough time in his marriage," this excuse is also a notch below "He's separated." Use this excuse and you may find yourself awkwardly trying to describe what exactly it is that you mean by "going through."

➡ HIS WIFE IS GOING TO SCREW HIM OVER IN THE DIVORCE, ANYWAY

Proceed with extreme caution here. For every girlfriend who might lend a sympathetic ear as you describe the demon wife, there's another who has herself been labeled the demon wife. Plus, feminist friends may reject your argument completely once you start knocking demon wives who are now saddled with the spawn of your new man-friend.

➡ WE'RE CONSENTING ADULTS

To a point, yes. But isn't there one other adult whose consent you are forgetting to count?

➦ WHAT SHE DOESN'T KNOW WON'T HURT HER

And in this great big world of adult indiscretions, how many affairs can you think of that haven't eventually been revealed somehow or another?

Exacerbating the problem is that, depending on your tone of voice, this excuse can come across as a dare. You may consciously or subconsciously enjoy the risk of your relationship, but do you really want your confidant feeling the temptation to share the story with the *other* other woman—as in the one with the ring?

➦ THE TWO-STATE-DISTANCE RULE

If you are new to infidelity, you might not be familiar with the two-state rule. The theory behind it is that it's okay to cheat on a significant other provided that there is enough of a geographic buffer between your homestead and the location of your indiscretion. Live in Oklahoma and have an affair with someone in Texas—not okay. Live in Michigan and hook up with someone in Louisiana, that's fine and dandy.

There are a number of factors that can make the two-state rule a messy philosophy on which to build your love life. For one, the two-state rule implies uniformity among the states. But as anyone with even a rudimentary geographical knowledge of the great U.S. of A. knows, you can skip over some states in a lunch hour (yes, we're looking at you, Delaware). Others take longer. As such, we don't think the two-state rule demonstrates the consistency that should make it a universally accepted law.

But let's not get too far off the interstate, so to speak. What you are really saying by evoking the two-state rule is that you are okay with having a relationship on the side as long as you don't let it interfere with his established daily life. You are saying that the relationship he's having with you can be kept in a box and that you won't step over any boundaries. Good luck with that.

➡ IT'S A MARRIAGE IN NAME ONLY

This implies that you know the deal that has evolved between the spouses in question. If you are confident that both other parties are on the same page about this, then you might be okay in some circles.

So why don't you give her a call and ask?

➡ HIS WIFE HAS PUT ON A LOT OF WEIGHT.

Congratulations! You have gained entrance to a special place in hell reserved just for bimbos like you.

ADDITIONAL EXCUSES FOR
being the
OTHER WOMAN

➤ WE MEANT TO TELL HER, BUT WE FORGOT.

➤ WE MEANT TO TELL HER, BUT SHE WAS SLEEPING AND WE DIDN'T WANT TO WAKE HER.

➤ WE MEANT TO TELL HER, BUT SHE WAS IN A COMA.

➤ I MEANT TO TELL HER, BUT I WAS TURNED INTO A PILLAR OF SALT.

➤ **SHE CAN'T HANDLE THE TRUTH!**

➤ **THOSE MAURY POVICH EPISODES AREN'T GOING TO WRITE THEMSELVES.**

➤ **WE'RE THINKING ABOUT CONVERTING TO MORMONISM. NOT THE NEW, SOCIALLY ACCEPTABLE KIND, BUT THE OLD-SCHOOL KIND. OF COURSE, WE HAVE A FEW STEPS TO GO—LIKE TELLING HIS WIFE.**

··· EXCUSES FOR BEING ···
PASSED OVER
FOR A JOB

Finding a job can be a painful and humiliating process. You dress up. You look good. You've rehearsed what you want to say. You answer questions with both a smile and the right degree of seriousness. It's all kind of like going on a first date.

Which could be why being rejected feels so awful.

It can be just as bad, if not worse, when a job opens up at a company where you already work. Eyes turn to you as a natural candidate for the position … but for some reason, you don't get it.

Here are a few excuses you might be tempted to take to the water cooler:

➡ I GUESS I WASN'T THE RIGHT "MAN" FOR THE JOB

Ah, yes. Throwing down the "It's still a man's world" gauntlet. More popular and believable twenty or thirty years ago, it's becoming less and less easy to use as more and more women find themselves in higher-up positions at the workplace.

So, before you use it, make sure that most of the high-paying jobs at this particular place of employment are occupied by men. And, while you are at it, make sure there aren't other jobs there that you might want to apply for later.

➡ AGEISM

Similar to the sexism call—and perhaps more prevalent today—ageism does keep many experienced workers out of jobs. The assumption is that those who were born prior to the Reagan administration will either demand too high a salary, expect too much deference, or won't be able to handle the latest technology.

Summoning this excuse, though, may lead to an unwanted question: "So how old are you exactly?"

➡ MY BOSS IS AN IDIOT

This is a nice catch-all to use privately—especially with people who also believe that your boss is an idiot. Watch for spies, though.

➡ I DON'T KISS ASS

This is a good, nonspecific excuse that will leave most of your coworkers nodding their heads in agreement. The problem comes, though, when word of your Norma Rae act gets back to the person who does get the job—who may well be pissed at the "kiss-ass" label you've pinned on him or her.

➡ THAT'S WHAT I GET FOR BEING TOO GOOD AT MY CURRENT POSITION

There is a theory, known as the Peter Principle, that states that people rise to their own level of incompetence. In other words, workers will continue to be promoted until they are in a job that they can't handle.

Then they stay there.

So maybe, just maybe, your boss is a wise one, making sure that a valuable employee doing a valuable job doesn't get Peter Principled into failing.

All of which makes this a good excuse that not only makes you look good, but makes your boss look wise. Unfortunately, none of that adds up to extra money in your paycheck.

➡ I LIKE WHERE I AM RIGHT NOW

This is a nice, cup-half-full way of looking at your situation. Even if this isn't how you really feel, people will smile at your optimism and sense of well-being. As for your resentment and feelings of failure, you can just keep pushing those down. Way down.

ADDITIONAL EXCUSES FOR BEING
PASSED OVER
FOR A JOB

➤ IT WAS PASSOVER.

➤ MAYBE I SHOULDN'T HAVE BELCHED THE NATIONAL ANTHEM AT MY REVIEW.

➤ MAYBE I SHOULDN'T HAVE SUGGESTED THE CREATION OF "DRESS AS YOUR FAVORITE UNION ORGANIZER DAY."

➤ MAYBE I SHOULD STOP TRYING TO STRONG-ARM COWORKERS INTO BUYING MY KID'S FUNDRAISING WRAPPING PAPER, CANDLES, MAGAZINE SUBSCRIPTIONS, NO-NAME CANDY BARS, CHEESE-AND-SAUSAGE TRAYS, GENERIC LAWN AND LEAF BAGS, AND COOKIE DOUGH. (BUT THERE'S A SIGN-UP SHEET BY THE COFFEEMAKER JUST IN CASE YOU'RE INTERESTED.)

➤ I SHOULDN'T HAVE SPENT A WEEK TRYING OUT MOST OF THE ENTRIES IN "THE UNDERGROUND MANUAL OF OFFICE DARES," ANOTHER FABULOUS BOOK FROM CIDER MILL PRESS. ASK FOR IT FROM YOUR FRIENDLY NEIGHBORHOOD BOOKSELLER.

➤ MY BOSS HAS NO SENSE OF HUMOR. BESIDES, IT'S NOT MY FAULT HE DIDN'T CHECK THE TOILET SEAT FOR SUPER GLUE BEFORE HE SAT DOWN.

➤ I PREFER TO SLEEP MY WAY TO THE TOP.

EXCUSES FOR DISAPPOINTING your BOOK CLUB

The premise is a simple and noble one: Gather friends, acquaintances, or even strangers together to share thoughts—whether intellectual or emotional—on a book that all have read. Inspired by Oprah Winfrey and fueled by a feeling that post-college human interaction should go beyond bar chat, family matters, movie talk, and complaining about work, book clubs allow (in theory) a respite from the mundane world in a nurturing environment.

So why are such gatherings rife with guilt and excuses? And why do so many women blow off the single-book-every-couple-of-weeks assignment? Here's the Cliff Notes version:

➡ I DIDN'T LIKE THE SELECTION

You're preaching to the choir here. Most books aren't designed to be enjoyed by the kind of cross-section of folks that have joined your book club. That would be too easy.

Keep in mind that, when someone in a book club recommends a book, she is most likely a.) trying to impress you, b.) trying to avoid the reading assignment by calling out a book that she has already read, or c.) trying to elevate her self-image by suggesting a book that she read a review of somewhere that will sound impressive in the retelling. "I heard about it in the *New York Times Book Review . . .*"

All of which is to say that, if you didn't like the selection, you're not alone. And that is a perfectly good excuse not to finish it. After all, there isn't a test. If you find yourself not reading any of the selections that your book club reads, maybe it's time to join a bowling team instead.

➡ I BARELY HAVE TIME TO BREATHE, LET ALONE READ

Nobody has time to read. Work, housework, and family take up so much time. And so do watching reality TV shows, Facebooking, shopping, texting, Twittering . . .

➡ I COULDN'T RELATE TO THE CHARACTERS

We don't mean to be insulting here, but do you really want to read a book about someone with your life? Bridget Jones, that last part was not directed at you.

➤ I SKIMMED IT

So did everyone else—including the critic who wrote the review that inspired that one woman in your group to recommend the crappy book in the first place.

➤ I'M JUST HERE TO GET OUT OF THE HOUSE

So is everyone else. And you know why? Nobody cares whether you read the book or not. Nobody cares if you were too busy or couldn't relate to the characters. Do you know what they care about? They care about the quality of the dip you brought to the meeting.

So, instead of anguishing over your lack of reading time, remember that it's always okay to blow off the last few chapters—or the entire book—to spend some time cooking something that will get everyone's minds off having botched the assignment.

ADDITIONAL EXCUSES FOR
..... disappointing .....
YOUR BOOK CLUB

➤➤ WELL, NOBODY LISTENED WHEN I SUGGESTED "HOP ON POP."

➤➤ I'M A BORN-AGAIN DYSLEXIC.

➤➤ BOOKS ARE SO PASSÉ.

➤➤ MY BOOKMARK GOT STUCK.

➤➤ I AM TOO PROUD AND PREJUDICED TO READ.

➤➤ I AM TERRIFIED OF PAPER CUTS.

➤➤ SORRY I COULDN'T MAKE IT. I HAD TO ATTEND A BOOK BURNING.

➤➤ LIBRARIES GIVE ME THE CREEPS.

········ EXCUSES FOR ········
BREAKING UP

Yes, Neil Sedaka was right: Breaking up is hard to do. And Paul Simon had it right when he declared that there must be fifty ways to leave your lover.

Of course, neither of those guys would have been any match for Gloria Gaynor when she declared "I Will Survive" in the wake of an ugly breakup.

The problem for the rest of us is that breakups rarely come with clever rhymes and back-up musicians. They come with frustration and anguish and heartbreak—ideally, not yours.

When you are in the position of having to deliver the news rather than get it (breaking up is certainly a situation where it's better to give than to receive, if only because you have the element of surprise), then sometimes excuses are in order. Here are some of the frequent outs:

➡ THIS IS WHAT'S BEST FOR BOTH OF US

Yes, but only one of you is making the decision. Don't expect the person who is getting this news flash to really think you have their best interests at heart. Or that you have a heart at all.

➡ I'VE JUST BEEN FEELING SO DISCONNECTED LATELY, AND I DON'T KNOW WHY

We'll tell you why: because you are tired of being saddled with this loser and want to move on to greener pastures. Or maybe you are already in those greener pastures. Maybe you've been in them for a long time and haven't told your partner. Maybe those greener pastures include a handsome stable boy named Lance who knows how to whisper to horses . . .

But we're getting carried away. The point is, he (your soon-to-be-ex, not the stable boy Lance) knows that you've felt disconnected. He probably felt disconnected, too. Only he was clearly more interested in actually being connected to you than you were in being connected to him.

➡ YOU ARE TOO GOOD FOR ME

This attempt to shoulder all the negative in a relationship has become so cliché that even if there were some sincerity in it—even if you actually believed that the dumpee was a catch too perfect to keep, and we all know that's a situation that will never occur in nature—it wouldn't make you sound any less like the bad guy.

On the contrary, it might actually help prove that your ex- was actually too good for you.

➡ IT'S NOT YOU, IT'S ME

Of course it's you. You're the one who is unhappy enough in this relationship that you have chosen to call it quits. But in the scene where you
deliver the break-up news to him, the wording folds back over on itself
like a Möbius strip and sounds something like this: "It's not you, it's me.
And I just don't like you."

If only life were a book on Border's Staff Picks shelf. We might be
able to travel romantically through time, to the point in the future when
your partner is involved in another relationship and realizes that, yes, it
was you.

➡ I THINK WE'RE BETTER AS FRIENDS

The problem with this excuse is that it has many possible translations.
You could be saying that you like everything about this guy, but you
aren't interested in the relationship being physical. You could be saying
that you think an emotional, romantic relationship is a bad idea, but
you would still like to hang on to the physical. Or you could be saying
that you are just filling air-time until you can get out of the room or
(shame on you) get off the phone.

➡ IT'S WHAT'S BEST FOR THE KIDS

The fallback of amicable divorcees everywhere, the helping-out-the-kids
excuse does occasionally, sometimes, once-in-a-great-while hold some
water. Is it really healthy for children to witness their venom-spouting,
separate-room-sleeping, bitterness-at-every-turn mom and dad trying to
pretend that everything in the house is hunky-dory? Isn't you-take-them-
on-weekends-and-I'll-manage-them-during-the-week preferable to flying toasters and acid tongues? We say yes, and so do our therapists.

The reality, though, is that even if you're up for Mother of the Year, you aren't separating because it's best for the kids. You're separating because you can't stand to live with each other anymore.

➡ I JUST NEED SOME TIME OFF

Careful with this one, because your jilted paramour is likely to demand specifics about why you are suddenly feeling so independent. You might also want to have a quick and convincing comeback for the possible response, "I'll wait for you."

➡ YOU'RE JUST NOT MY TYPE

The effectiveness of this one depends on at what point in the relationship it's being brought to your partner's attention. After a few get-to-know-each-other dates, it can be a fairly easy way to be nonspecific and noninsulting. Unfortunately, some people don't suffer the wishy-washy gladly. They want to know why. And there you have to tread carefully.

➥ WE'RE TWO DIFFERENT PEOPLE

Of course you are. At some point, did you think you were amoeba?

➥ I SAW YOU WITH THAT OTHER GIRL

This one has some pull. Even more so if you can say, "I saw you with your hands on that other girl's butt," or "I saw that other girl's car parked in your driveway at three o'clock in the morning." Just be ready to hear some sort of "perfectly logical" rebuttal like, "She just needed someone to talk to, and I was there for her. I'm sorry if you misunderstood."

➥ I'VE MET SOMEBODY ELSE

Hopefully, you have already removed all of your CDs from his apartment when you deliver this punch.

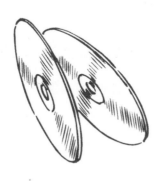

ADDITIONAL EXCUSES FOR
BREAKING UP

➤ **ACCORDING TO THE DNA TESTS, SURPRISE, WE'RE COUSINS!**

➤ **I'M CONVERTING TO A RELIGION INCOMPATIBLE WITH YOURS.**

➤ **DATING YOU CUTS INTO MY SOCIAL NETWORKING TIME.**

➤ **I'VE LONG BEEN HARBORING A RESENTMENT ABOUT THAT ONE TIME WHEN YOU CUT ME OFF.**

➤ **I'M A CAT PERSON. YOU'RE A DOG PERSON.**

➤ **YOU DON'T WANT TO CATCH WHAT I HAVE!**

➤ **I'M ALL HUGGED OUT.**

➤ **IT'S RESEARCH FOR MY NEW CAREER AS A COUNTRY MUSIC WRITER.**

➤ **IT'S A UNION THING.**

➤ **FAIRER SEX, MY ASS.**

➤ **YOU ARE A LITTLE HEAVIER THAN YOUR AVATAR WOULD SUGGEST.**

EXCUSES FOR
COMPROMISING
PHOTOS

The combination of the Internet and cell phone technology has created possibilities that Sean Connery (or even Roger Moore) could only have dreamed of.

But for all their good, these rapid, user-friendly media have one major downside: If there are naked pictures of you somewhere . . . anywhere . . . there is an exponentially greater chance now than in any other time in the history of communication technology that everyone you ever knew will see your boobs. (Sorry, Dad!)

The trick, of course, is to not have them taken at all. Unfortunately, we don't always have that kind of foresight.

So what do you say when an innocent nude photo session with your ex—or a not-so-innocent video you decided to shoot just to see what you look like doin' it—gets sent around the globe, right into the inboxes of your friends, family, and coworkers? You reach for a cover-up.

➡ THAT WAS SUPPOSED TO JUST BE FOR US

Unless your name is Jenna Jameson, you really do mean this. You would not be the first girl to want to do something nice for the two of you, something a little sexy and dangerous to spice things up a little bit. But rather than showing your innocence, you are showing your idiocy.

➡ SOMEBODY HAD A CAMERA PHONE

Okay, the bigger question might be: Why were you doing that while he (or she) was making a phone call?

➡ HE WAS AN ARTIST

Very few artists only use one camera angle.

➡ I WAS YOUNG

Youth can be an acceptable excuse the further away you get from it.

➡ I WAS DRUNK

Save this excuse and use it only among other people who have also done very stupid things while inebriated.

➡ SOMEDAY, YEARS FROM NOW, WHEN I'M NOT NEARLY THIS HOT, I'LL BE HAPPY THAT I PRESERVED AN IMAGE OF ME WHEN I HAD IT ALL TOGETHER

And millions of guys at their laptops behind locked doors are really happy about that, too.

ADDITIONAL EXCUSES FOR
COMPROMISING
PHOTOS

➤➤ IT'S BEEN AIRBRUSHED ANYWAY.

➤➤ I WAS OFFERED CANDY. I LIKE CANDY.

➤➤ I THOUGHT THE LENS CAP WAS ON.

➤➤ THEY MAY HAVE CAPTURED MY IMAGE,
BUT THEY'LL NEVER CAPTURE MY SOUL.

➤ IT WORKS AT MARDI GRAS. WHY WOULDN'T IT WORK AT TIFFANY'S?

➤ I'M TRYING TO GET ADOPTED BY THE KARDASHIANS.

➤ I LIKE TO BE THE BREAST THAT I CAN BE.

➤ WHOOOOOOOOOOO! SPRING BREAK!

➤ THERE WAS A NIP IN THE AIR.

EXCUSES FOR
COMPROMISING YOUR DREAMS

We're in big-picture territory now, looking back to a point in your life when you had big plans. When hope was high. When ideals were strong. When the future was a great big highway with lots of very cool exits. And every one of those exits had easy on/off access so you could take that exit, see if you liked what you found there, and, if you didn't, get back on that great big wonderful highway and explore other great big wonderful futures.

Now that the future looks like not much more than the path between home, work, the Subway sandwich shop on the corner, and home; when you've rationalized another compromise; and when you come to the conclusion that not only haven't you "shown" all the people you said "I'll show you," but you aren't ever going to show them anything . . .

Let's stop right there. We're starting to depress ourselves. Because we really intended to write a novel. Not just a novel, a great novel. Perhaps the great American novel.

But then these Excuses projects came along and we're making the same excuses you might be, including:

➡ I NEEDED TO EAT

The usefulness of this excuse depends largely on how big your dreams were in the first place. If they were big big, it is doubtful that any mortal soul could have reached them. Then, it's perfectly understandable to most people why the need for sustenance took you down a different path.

If you are using it to explain why you gave up on that dream of yours to read a book a month, then it's not going to fly.

➡ I NEEDED THE BENEFITS

Even more so sometimes than money, the need for insurance stability can be an acceptable out for taking a thankless job far, far from your college major. Feel free to use this excuse, as you enjoy your six-month checkup at the dentist or co-pay for a prescription of antibiotics . . . but keep the dream alive.

➡ I HAD A HUSBAND AND KIDS TO WORRY ABOUT

This one can pass with some people. But with your stronger-willed female friends, the follow-up might be, "Yeah, so how much did he compromise?"

➡ I NEVER REALLY HAD ANY TALENT

Here's a perfectly good excuse if, in fact, you didn't actually have any talent. If you did, though, and the people you are using it on know that, then you are just sending out invitations to a pity party.

➡ MY COLLEGE DIDN'T REALLY PREPARE ME

That's where things like diligence, fortitude, and other you-go-girl traits come in handy. Blaming your college will only get you so far . . . unless it's Temple University or Ball State University, the institutions of higher learning that we attended. If either of those are the case, then go ahead and blame away. We do it all the time.

➡ THIS TOWN REALLY ISN'T SO BAD

The dream of getting out of a dead-end town is a common one (and the source of fully one-eighth of all Bruce Springsteen lyrics).

The reality that most of the world isn't any better—and contains a lot more strangers—doesn't seem important when you are in your late teens or early twenties. Once you're a full-fledged adult, though, it's not necessarily a compromise to appreciate what's in your own back yard. It worked for Dorothy. It worked for George Bailey. It might actually work for you.

ADDITIONAL EXCUSES FOR
COMPROMISING YOUR DREAMS

➤ OH, THOSE DREAMS? THEY WERE ALL JUST THE RESULTS OF SOME REALLY BAD LSD.

➤ OH, THOSE DREAMS? THEY WERE JUST MY PARENTS' DREAMS. THEY WANTED MORE FROM ME THAN I WANT FROM ME. I'M HAPPY. NOW PASS THE DAMN FUNYONS.

➤ OH, THOSE DREAMS? I JUST DREAMED THEM.

➤ I DON'T REMEMBER MY DREAMS. I THINK I'LL PAY A FAKE PARAPSYCHOLOGIST A LOT OF MONEY TO TELL ME WHAT MY DREAMS ARE AND THEN I WILL HAVE A CLEARER IDEA OF WHAT I'M BLOWING OFF.

EXCUSES FOR
COOKING
(NOT)

We know it's cheaper to cook a home-cooked meal. We know it's healthier to eat a home-cooked meal. We know it saves time to eat a home-cooked meal. But there's a big problem with a home-cooked meal. It requires cooking at home.

And as much as we admire Julia Child and worship at the altar of the Food Network, we've long ago changed our definition of "cooking" to mean "heating something up." Actual cooking—the combining of ingredients in the preparation of a meal—doesn't happen nearly as often as it should.

And, of course, we feel guilty about it. So, we try excuses like the following:

➡ THERE WAS NOTHING IN THE FRIDGE

Yes, there was. But there's only so much you can do with vodka, unused soy sauce packets, an egg, half a Panera sandwich, and a piece of fruit formerly known as a peach.

➡ I WAS OUT OF EGGS

That's why God created neighbors. And supermarkets. And convenience stores.

➡ I DIDN'T WANT TO DIRTY UP THE KITCHEN

This makes sense . . . if you also avoid sleeping under your sheets in the bedroom, making an actual fire in your fireplace, showering in your bathroom, or otherwise sullying your model home.

➡ WITH A COUPON, IT'S CHEAPER TO EAT OUT

At some eateries, perhaps. But how many Whoppers do you really want to eat this week—or in one sitting? (Don't answer that.)

➡ SUPERMARKETS ANNOY ME

That could be because you haven't used them enough to understand how they work. It's simple, really:

1. You look for the food you want.
2. You take it to the check-out.
3. You pay for it.
4. Repeat as often as necessary.

➡ I LOST MY LOYALTY CARD

They have more. Just ask and surely your loyalty will be welcomed back.

➡ WE HAD A POWER FAILURE

Now you are starting to enter the dangerous territory of the fact-checkable excuse. Also, be aware before using this that just after a power failure is often the best time to use your kitchen—wouldn't want all of that previously frozen or refrigerated food to spoil, would you?

➡ IT'S DOING THE DISHES THAT GETS TO ME

They get to everyone. But there's also this new thing called a dishwasher. A real labor-saver. Look for it under your kitchen counter.

➡ I WAS OUT OF FLOUR

We may be wrong here, but aren't there at least a thousand recipes that don't require flour? (Not that we've actually tried too many of them.)

ADDITIONAL EXCUSES FOR
COOKING (NOT)

➤ **MY APARTMENT DOESN'T HAVE A KITCHEN.**

➤ **FOOD IS SO PASSÉ.**

➤ **WHAT DO I LOOK LIKE, DONNA REED?**

➤ **BECAUSE OLIVE IS SO MUCH BETTER OF A COOK THAN ME. YOU KNOW, OLIVE GARDEN.**

➤ **NOTE TO SELF: UNWRAP THE ENGLISH CUCUMBER BEFORE SLICING IT.**

➤ **I'M TRYING THE SUBWAY DIET.**

➤ **I DON'T KNOW HOW TO CHANGE THE CHANNEL ON MY OVEN.**

➤ **MY CRISPER DRAWER IS STUCK.**

➤ **YOU WANT TO KNOW WHAT'S BETTER THAN ROBERT REDFORD? ORDERING PIZZA.**

··EXCUSES FOR BEING A··
CRAZY EX-GIRLFRIEND

The crazy ex-girlfriend is as much an iconic figure in our times as the stalwart cowboy and the grizzled prospector were in theirs. The difference is that the stalwart cowboy and the grizzled prospector never tried to key a guy's freshly painted car, put tuna fish sandwiches in his mail slot while he was on vacation, pee in his shampoo bottle, or issue warning e-mails to his latest squeeze.

What excuse could there possibly be for being that crazy ex-girlfriend? History has shown that there have been many, some more valid than others.

➡ AFTER WHAT HE DID TO ME . . .

Yes, revenge can be sweet. And the greater the infraction from your ex, the more likely that your friends (and, possibly, the courts) will accept his bad (unprompted) behavior as an excuse for your bad (prompted) actions.

Make sure, of course, that those you are explaining yourself to have an equally bad image of your ex—and that any exaggeration you might be making to firm up support can't be contradicted by available facts or trusted sources.

➡ IT'S NOT MY FAULT I KNEW ALL OF HIS PASSWORDS

Good luck with this one. Just because you can get onto his social networking sites or into his e-mail or bank account doesn't mean that you should get onto his social networking sites and into his e-mail and bank accounts.

➡ I STILL HAD THE KEY

Similar to the above, having the key doesn't mean permission to enter. And remember, it's going to be pretty clear to everyone in both of your social circles (and the police) who is responsible for spray painting "Jerk Face" on his living room wall and putting his best ties through his paper shredder.

➡ HE'S LUCKY I DIDN'T DO WORSE

Perhaps. And you're lucky he didn't press charges. Yet.

➨ HE REALLY DOES STILL LOVE ME, NO MATTER WHAT HE SAID

A dark corner of refuge for the wronged woman is to assume you know better than he does what he is feeling. Really, we are just as hard-pressed to think of an instance in which this justification is true as we are to think of a situation in which uttering these words will not make you sound desperately misguided in the very best light and mentally unbalanced in the very worst.

➨ HIS WIFE IS RUINING HIS LIFE— HE DESERVES BETTER

This reasoning doesn't hold much water when it's used as an excuse for being the other woman. It's even lamer when it's being used by the crazy ex other woman.

➨ THE TATTOO IS MEANT TO REMEMBER THE GOOD TIMES [AND/OR] SO I DON'T MAKE THE SAME MISTAKE AGAIN

That might be what you think it means. The message it sends, however, is that you are toxic, and that the ten-foot pole that other guys won't touch you with might be a few yards too short.

➨ IT WORKS IN THE MOVIES

This ain't the movies.

ADDITIONAL EXCUSES FOR BEING
A CRAZY EX-GIRLFRIEND

➤ GUYS DIG CRAZY EX-GIRLFRIENDS. IT SHOWS THAT WE UNDERSTAND COMMITMENT.

➤ IF I STAY OBSESSED WITH THE GUY WHO DUMPED ME AND DEVOTE MY LIFE TO WINNING HIM BACK, I WON'T EVER HAVE TO WORRY ABOUT AWKWARD, EMBARRASSING REBOUND SEX WITH ANOTHER GUY.

➤ IT BEATS BEING A CRAZY GIRLFRIEND BECAUSE CRAZY GIRLFRIENDS REQUIRE GIFTS FOR THEIR BIRTHDAYS AND MAJOR HOLIDAYS.

➤ I'M NOT CRAZY. I'M COMPLEX.

➤ DID HE CALL YOU? SERIOUSLY, DID HE? WHAT DID HE SAY? DID HE SAY ANYTHING ABOUT ME? DID HE SAY ANYTHING ABOUT US? NOT THAT I CARE. BUT WHAT DID HE SAY? SERIOUSLY, WHAT DID HE SAY? I JUST WANT TO KNOW WHAT HE'S SAYING. WHAT HE'S SAYING ABOUT ME. I HAVE A RIGHT TO KNOW, DON'T I? DON'T YOU THINK I HAVE A RIGHT TO KNOW? CALL ME RIGHT BACK WHEN YOU GET THIS MESSAGE, OKAY?

➤ EVER SINCE ALIENATING MYSELF FROM MY FRIENDS AND FAMILY, I'VE HAD A LOT OF FREE TIME ON MY HANDS.

➤ THE BASEBALL BAT SLIPPED . . . SO MAN UP. IT'S STILL DRIVABLE.

➤ I GAVE HIM THE BEST TWO WEEKS OF MY LIFE!

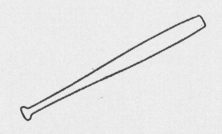

EXCUSES FOR THE
DAY AFTER

Morning already? It seems like just a few hours ago you were...? What exactly was it that you were doing? And how did you end up with that incoherent Sharpie-writing on your arm? And what was that guy's name again? And whose digits are those in your cell phone? And where are your keys? And how much is it going to cost to replace those barstools?

When the previous night is a blur, the day ahead looks to be a headache, and the hair of the dog that bit you isn't helping your hangover, it's time for a new batch of remedy excuses. Here are some common ones to help you through the fog:

➡ I WAS DRINKING TEQUILA

So were a lot of people the world over, my friend. And assuming you are all grown-ups who can handle your liquor, none of you should be surprised at the results of an evening spent in its company.

➡ MY SHOES WERE KILLING ME

Standard response number one from a husband/boyfriend: "Are you trying to tell me you don't have any shoes in that overstuffed closet that actually fit?"

Standard response number two from a husband/boyfriend: "You mean to tell me you spent two hours getting dressed and you still ended up with the wrong ones?"

Standard response number three from a husband/boyfriend: "So is that any reason to throw them at a cop?"

➡ I DIDN'T HAVE A SOBER BUDDY

This excuse indicates that in the past, you really needed a sober buddy. Which makes you look even worse this time around because, if you have been down this road before, then it was incumbent on you to make sure you had a sober buddy with you before you proved that you needed a sober buddy.

On the other hand, practice makes perfect.

➡ THAT'S WHAT YOU'RE SUPPOSED TO DO AT A BACHELORETTE PARTY

Yes, for a certain realm of brides-to-be, the bachelorette party offers the same special dispensation as those of a bachelor party.

Nonetheless, you should be careful about such evidence-gathering devices as cell-phone cameras. What happens in Vegas can only stay in Vegas if it doesn't find its way onto YouTube.

➡ YOU ONLY GO TO SPRING BREAK ONCE— OKAY, MAYBE TWICE

Just remember: Spring breaks are gone in the blink of an eye. But Girls Gone Wild DVDs are forever.

➡ I NEEDED TO DE-STRESS

Who can't relate to the need to relieve tension? Who doesn't feel overwhelmed by the burdens of the world? This universality helps this excuse rise to a level of success with all but the most extreme situations.

➡ EVEN THE AMISH ARE ALLOWED TO GO NUTS ONCE

The expression is "Are you ready to rumble?" not, "Are you ready to rumspringa?"

➡ WE WERE OFF THE CLOCK

It has been said that the problem with office parties is finding a new job the next day. Your work pals might have been laughing the loudest when you lapsed into the impromptu lap dance at the sloppy end of your company's holiday gathering, but they are not going to be there at your side when you get the stomach-unraveling e-mail from your boss in the morning, asking you to come up and chat.

ADDITIONAL EXCUSES FOR
THE DAY AFTER

➤ IT'S NOT THE DAY AFTER BECAUSE I NEVER WENT TO BED.

➤ AT LEAST I FOUND MY WAY HOME. THAT SHOULD COUNT FOR SOMETHING.

➤ I'M NOT SAYING ANYTHING BECAUSE 1.) I DON'T NEED TO EXPLAIN MYSELF TO YOU, AND 2.) MY HEAD HURTS TOO MUCH WHEN I TALK.

➤ REMEMBER THAT MADE-FOR-TV MOVIE CALLED "THE DAY AFTER"? IT WAS ABOUT PEOPLE TRYING TO SURVIVE IN A POST-NUCLEAR-BOMB WORLD? WELL, WHATEVER I DID COULDN'T BE AS BAD AS THAT.

➤ MY PAROLE OFFICER SHOULD HAVE KNOWN BETTER.

···EXCUSES FOR DOING···
A DRIVE-BY

We've all been there. And by "there," we mean hunched behind the steering wheel of our car, in a neighborhood not our own, sometime between the hours of midnight and 3 a.m. We are not exactly sure what we are looking for when we slow to an idle in front of his house. An incriminating car in the driveway? A silhouette against the bedroom blinds? Lingerie strewn across the lawn? But when and if we find it, there will be hell to pay, Mister I'm-just-going-to-stay-in-tonight-and-catch-up-on-my-Netflix. But if, God forbid, you are the one who gets caught in the act, you'd better have a good story.

➡ YOU WEREN'T PICKING UP THE PHONE

So disregard the seventeen voicemail messages.

➡ I JUST WANTED TO MAKE SURE YOU WERE OKAY

That's right. Switch the focus of concern to the other person—the one who isn't sporting blood-shot eyes, pajama bottoms, and a nervous tic due to lack of sleep. The faux concern might draw attention away from your own infirmities long enough for you to check his collar for lipstick.

➡ I WAS IN THE NEIGHBORHOOD

Shopping at the 24-hour retribution store, of course.

➡ MY GPS SCREWED UP

And you didn't stop to ask for directions? Busted!

➡ I THOUGHT I LEFT SOMETHING AT YOUR HOUSE

Let's see . . . would that be your curling iron or your dignity?

➡ IT'S A FREE COUNTRY

Yeah, okay, kind of. But have fun at tax time.

ADDITIONAL EXCUSES FOR
DOING A DRIVE-BY

➤ THERE'S NOWHERE ELSE ON EARTH THAT I WOULD RATHER BE.

➤ I JUST WANTED TO MAKE SURE THE DOGS WERE OKAY. WE DID HAVE DOGS, DIDN'T WE? I SEEM TO REMEMBER DOGS.

➤ OH, THAT WAS HIS STREET?

IF I DELIBERATELY DIDN'T DRIVE BY, THEN THAT WOULD SHOW THAT I'M STILL IMPACTED BY HIS ABSENCE. THE FACT THAT I DROVE BY SHOWS THAT I CAN HANDLE DRIVING BY HIS PLACE AND THAT I'M NOT GOING OUT OF MY WAY TO AVOID THAT PARTICULAR STREET, WHICH IS A GOOD SIGN, ISN'T IT? SERIOUSLY, IT'S A GOOD SIGN. YOU HAVE TO SEE THAT. YOU HAVE TO. BECAUSE, WHAT? I'M NOT SUPPOSED TO EVER, EVER GO DOWN HIS STREET? LIKE HIS STREET IS GOING TO BRING UP ALL KINDS OF, LIKE, NEGATIVE ENERGY OR SOMETHING? SORRY, BUT I CAN HANDLE GOING DOWN HIS STREET. AND I'LL PROVE IT TO YOU. I'LL DRIVE DOWN HIS STREET TONIGHT. AND TOMORROW NIGHT. AND THE NEXT NIGHT, AND YOU'LL SEE THAT I CAN HANDLE IT. REALLY.

EXCUSES FOR FASHION MISTAKES

Fashion has been around since people first began laying out clothes that were more coordinating than fig leaves and pelts to protect them from the elements.

Argue all you want about the damage that can come with idolizing the hollow-eyed, cigarette-thin models of the Prada runway. We're not out to bash little girls' collective self-esteem here. All we are saying is looking fabulous is one thing. Looking like you didn't just roll out of bed and into your dirty laundry hamper is a whole other ball of tube socks.

➧ IT LOOKED REALLY CUTE IN "LUCKY" MAGAZINE

On the upside, you are referencing the fact that you read fashion magazines. You are up on all the urban cowboy, French Riviera, and fairy-inspired pieces that the editors at Conde Nast currently covet, and you have probably even made optimistic use of all those little "Yes" and "Maybe" stickers. On the downside, you have somehow glossed over the possibility that you, perhaps, are not a belted-denim-sundress-and-turquoise-pendant kind of girl.

➧ I SAW IT ON THE RED CARPET

Careful throwing around this pretext. The same celeb showcase that saw the likes of Salma Hayek's fabulous halter gown and Halle Berry's sexy one-shouldered Versace has also been the scene of crimes by Bjork, Lady Gaga, and whoever is picking out Meryl Streep's outfits these days. And Mary Hart won't be at your office holiday party with her *ET* microphone to let you explain away your fashion sins.

➧ I HATE WEARING THE SAME THING EVERY DAY

Variety might be the spice of life, but it is no excuse for pleather mini-skirts.

➧ I WAS IN A RUT

Just because you felt the need to bust out of your routine doesn't mean the person in the next cubicle should have to take anti-seizure medicine on the days you opt for neon and latex.

➡ IT'S LAUNDRY DAY

You might think that a reference to your sad and empty life would evoke empathy. It doesn't.

➡ I HAVE BAD LIGHTING AT HOME

Fool you once—shame on your bedroom fluorescents for making you think a midnight blue turtleneck would work with a black pencil skirt, or that your new pair of control-top hose would let you finally get away with a spandex mini dress. Fool you twice—shame on you!

➡ IT WASN'T SEE-THROUGH WHEN I PUT IT ON THIS MORNING

Which doesn't change the fact that you will have to wear your shame all day.

➡ I PAID A LOT OF MONEY FOR THIS

Expect the opposite of forgiveness if you admit that the cartoonish, over-designed getup you are wearing is also going to make you late on rent this month.

➡ NOTHING ELSE FITS ME ANYMORE

It is possible to get some mileage out of this excuse, especially if you can back it up with a medically induced transformation like bariatric surgery or some kind of thyroid condition. It does not, however, give you carte blanche to perpetually dip into your sweatpants drawer.

➡ IT SHRUNK IN THE WASH

Psssst, your denial is showing.

➡ ONLY NERDS TUCK IN THEIR SHIRTS

Nerds and people who haven't been eating three doughnuts for break-fast every morning for the past month.

➡ IT'S A DESIGNER LABEL

Designers make mistakes, too. One of their biggest mistakes is in thinking that we live in a size-two world, where all of God's creatures have legs up to their chins and bottoms that could fit into two teacups. In the real world that we live in, that leopard-print unitard with the purple suede knee boots makes you look like a hooker.

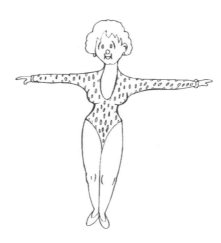

ADDITIONAL EXCUSES FOR
FASHION MISTAKES

➤ IT LOOKED GOOD ON MY EX. SO I TOOK IT. I DON'T REALLY LIKE IT, BUT I KNEW HE LIKED IT.

➤ I COULD'VE SWORN TODAY WAS DRESS LIKE A LOSER DAY.

➤ IT'S ALL THE RAGE IN KUALA LUMPUR.

➤ I'VE BEEN CAST IN A NEW REALITY SHOW ON A&E: "WEAR THE UGLIEST THING IN YOUR CLOSET." GOES ON THE AIR IN THE FALL.

➤ I AM UNCOORDINATED.

EXCUSES FOR GIVING AWAY A SECRET

We all want to think that we are trustworthy—that we are the kind of friend whom friends can have faith in. We are not gossipy like those other people.

That's not the story on the street. When it comes down to it, a secret burns in your brain. It requests . . . no, demands that you share it, lest it eat you alive. From the inside.

Of course, when you do give away a secret, you do it with the sincere hope that the person you are telling is trustworthy—the kind of friend whom friends can have faith in. Not a gossip like those other people (such as yourself).

And so it goes, until word gets back to the person who trusted you that the secret is out.

What could you possibly say? Well, maybe something like:

➡ PEOPLE WERE GOING TO FIND OUT ANYWAY

This excuse takes your personal responsibility for an action and pins it on the nature of the universe. A pretty gutsy move, don't you think? Even if you are right, you're not out of trouble.

➡ IT SLIPPED

It's true that sometimes you say something that you didn't mean to say. And sometimes that something is a deep, personal secret shared with you by a loyal friend. And sometimes you've undermined that whole relationship by not respecting him or her enough to be careful with your words. Don't think that a Bambi-eyed delivery of this excuse will make you look any less guilty.

➡ I DIDN'T MEAN TO SEND IT

The pesky "Enter/Return" keyboard button has caused more damage in its few decades of existence than the post office has ever done. Follow this one with a big "I'm sorry. I'm really, really sorry," and if the betrayal is a small one, you might just be given some grace.

Unfortunately, life does not have an "Apple/z" function.

➡ I WAS JUST TRYING TO HELP

When unattached to specifics, this excuse is a lame one. When piled high with details—plus a touch of genuine concern for the health and/or well being of the person you ratted on, you might just get off the hook.

➡ IT WAS NO BIG DEAL ANYWAY

That's it. Don't just betray the trust of your friend, but trivialize his or her problems as well. Nice way to double down.

ADDITIONAL EXCUSES FOR
GIVING AWAY A SECRET

➤ **I WAS TICKLED.**

➤ **I WAS WATERBOARDED.**

➤ **WE'RE ALL ONE PEOPLE AND WE SHOULDN'T KEEP SECRETS FROM ANYONE. KUMBAYA.**

EXCUSES FOR
PLAYING THE
GRANDMOTHER
card

Whether you are a Norman Rockwellish granny in her golden years, a young parent of a young parent, or anywhere in the decades between, your elevated status as grandparent makes you privy to a set of excuses developed especially for you.

➥ IT'S MY JOB TO SPOIL THEM

By this, you mean it's your job to make the kids' parents look like incompetent jerks. And the kids' parents know that this is the situation, because they remember full well how, back in their own halcyon days of grandparental spoiling, your parents made you look like a jerk.

One of the reasons this and other grandparent excuses are so effective is that there is little your adult kids can do to counter them. Nobody wants the reputation of being mean to grandma. So, while the excuse itself may be totally silly and invalid, it works because there's no system for it not working.

➥ I RAISED MY OWN CHILDREN. I DON'T HAVE TO RAISE YOURS

Three different grandmothers can use this same excuse in very different circumstances. For the hands-off grandmother with high expectations for children's behavior, it can be a way to expect ends without having to work on means. You fully expect your grandchildren to know which fork to use, how to fold sheets, etc. They should come to you with this knowledge, and it is up to the parents to educate them—even if they, themselves, don't hold the same values.

For the fun, fun, fun grandma—the one akin to the divorced dad— this is similar to the "I only see them once a year" excuse (see next excuse). It's a write-off for doing anything you damn well feel like doing with your grandkids—being their senior buddy—and then dumping them back with their parents when it's time to actually behave.

Finally, there's the grandma who is being saddled with the grandchildren because the kids' mom and/or dad want to live a more active life. They want to get out more. They want to party. They want to go rock climbing in the Andes or surfing in Malibu. And they figure why not just stick the kids with grandma. She's not doing anything. In all three circumstances, the score is: Advantage, Grandma.

➥ I ONLY SEE THEM ONCE A YEAR

This one works fairly well because it lets you do anything you damn well please while also giving the middlemen (the kids' parents) an out. Knowing that your indulgences are a special case makes reverting to normalcy a little bit easier.

➥ I DON'T KNOW WHAT THEY LIKE

This is a common excuse pulled out when a grandparent transitions from buying a gift for a grandchild that is either wrong or quickly broken into just sending a check or giving cash.

As if giving money really needs an excuse.

➥ IT WAS GOOD ENOUGH FOR US

Yes, maybe. But so were phones with cords, TVs that picked up only a dozen channels, pre-packaged meals that you actually cooked in an oven instead of a microwave, typewriters, Pong . . .

➥ SORRY, I DIDN'T HEAR YOU

Your ears may be as functional as they were forty years ago, but every senior knows that, once the hair turns gray, not having heard something becomes an effective, easy-to-use, impossible-to-respectfully-argue-with excuse.

ADDITIONAL EXCUSES FOR
PLAYING THE
GRANDMOTHER
·····card·····

➤ YOU ONLY WISH YOU REACHED
YOUR FORMATIVE YEARS IN THE
1940S/1950S/1960S/1970S/1980S.

➤ THAT'S HOW THINGS WERE IN THE
1940S/1950S/1960S/1970S/1980S.

➤ I'M STARTING A CONVENIENCE STORE
IN MY PURSE.

➤ I'VE EARNED EVERY PENNY OF MY FIXED
INCOME, AND I CAN SPEND IT AS I WISH. NOW
DOUBLE DOWN!

·······EXCUSES FOR·······
LATENESS/
NOT SHOWING UP

If you are like most people, you work best under pressure. When the clock is ticking toward 9 a.m., and you were supposed to be at your desk by 8:30. When you really, really don't want to go on that second date. When you just plain stood somebody up and now have some 'splaining to do. These are the times when your creative muscle is most flexible.

Of course, if you had put as much effort into showing up on time—or showing up at all—we wouldn't be having this discussion.

➡ I DIDN'T HAVE A THING TO WEAR

More to the point, you didn't have anything that would coordinate with your look of shame.

➡ I COULDN'T GET THE KIDS MOVING THIS MORNING

Audiences are generally sympathetic to the plight of a harried mother. They can just see you yanking the comforters off those lazy little rug rats, plucking the Wii's out of their hands, and chasing after them with their books and lunchboxes. So, you might get a kindly pardon if you peg the tardiness on your kids, the more ornery the better. If you don't actually have any kids . . . not so much.

➡ MY KID MISSED THE BUS

This one will work, but only once a semester.

➡ MY HUSBAND/BOYFRIEND DIDN'T PUT THE KEYS BACK WHERE THEY WERE SUPPOSED TO BE

Use this excuse, and then quickly segue into a rant about how "it's always the man's fault." This conversational U-turn will divert attention away from your own lack of consideration. But all bets are off if the person you are trying to sell on this concept is a man.

➡ I HAD TO STOP FOR PADS

Works like a charm when you really don't want the conversation to go any further.

➡ I COULDN'T GET A BABYSITTER

It's simple, sweet, and a testament to your high parental standards. Bonus points if you use this as an excuse for standing up your own babysitter.

➡ I HAVE TO WASH MY HAIR

Are Frenchy and Rizzo going to come over and pierce your ears as well?

➡ I HAVE TO GET UP EARLY TOMORROW

Even when it's true—especially when it's true—people will rarely buy this defense. If anything, it will throw fuel on the "c'mon, just for one drink" fire.

➡ IT WAS A SCHOOL NIGHT

And you, being a responsible person with textbooks to read and equations to study, stayed up until dawn watching *Buffy* DVDs.

➡ I WANTED TO BE FASHIONABLY LATE

Just so you know, being late isn't nearly as fashionable as gossiping about the person who is late.

➡ I WAS WAITING FOR THE CABLE GUY

Works fine, as long as you don't have a satellite dish.

ADDITIONAL EXCUSES FOR
LATENESS/
NOT SHOWING UP

➤➤ **I WAS TOO DRUNK TO READ MY WATCH.**

➤➤ **I'VE TAKEN PEYOTE AND TIME IS REALLY KIND OF MEANINGLESS RIGHT NOW.**

➤➤ **BEING LESS CONSTRAINED BY TIME COMMITMENTS IS PART OF MY ONGOING THERAPY.**

➤➤ **MY FLUX CAPACITOR BROKE.**

EXCUSES FOR
LAZINESS/
GENERAL SLOTH

We all have our to-do list. But sometimes motivation eludes the best of us. Conveniently, sleeping in until noon gives you plenty of time to dream up reasons why you aren't doing what you should be doing.

➡ I WORK ALL DAY

You haven't exactly cornered the market on the 9-to-5 day. So why would you expect fellow members of the workforce to cut you any slack when you play the drudgery card?

➡ THE PILL MAKES ME GAIN WEIGHT

Looking a little pudgy and couch potato-y all of a sudden? The medical community will back you up on the birth control–induced puffiness . . . to a degree. But nobody is going to write you a prescription for late-night Ben & Jerry binging or your aversion to the gym.

➡ I'M NOT VERY ATHLETIC

If you are using this excuse to fend off that pushy recruiter for the office softball team, then more power to you. (Who needs yet another reason to get reamed by an overzealous immediate supervisor with a high-five fetish?)

If, on the other hand, you are using this as some sort of note-from-the-doctor way of opting out of anything more physical than a walk down the driveway, then you should keep in mind that excuses and exercise go together like cellulite and Spandex. That is to say, not very well.

➤ I DIDN'T WANT TO RUIN MY NAILS

A fresh manicure is a terrible thing to waste. But there is only one person who exists in that fold in time when the fingernail polish is still a little wet and all physical contact with the world is put on hold, and that one person is you. If you're talking about the self-imposed prison of artificial nails or freakishly long talons (with or without the rhinestone embellishment), expect no mercy.

➤ I HAVE A HEADACHE

Everyone gets headaches. Therefore, everyone can identify with a fellow sufferer. By the same token, the universality of the condition could just as easily work against you. "It's just a little headache, for crying out loud," people will say—especially if those people are being asked to pick up your slack.

ADDITIONAL EXCUSES FOR
LAZINESS/
GENERAL SLOTH

➤ I WATCHED AN ENTIRE SEASON OF "HOUSE." DO YOU KNOW HOW EXHAUSTING THAT IS?

➤ IT'S MORE FUN GOING TO THE GYM IF IT'S A SURPRISE.

➤ I SPENT ALL DAY WORKING ON THE FARM ... WELL, ON FARMVILLE.

➤ OKAY, IT MIGHT BE ONE OF THE SEVEN DEADLY SINS. BUT IT'S NOT EVEN CLOSE TO THE TOP FIVE.

➤ THAT'S WHAT HUSBANDS ARE FOR.

EXCUSES FOR MISSING A PERIOD

Uh-oh. As much as you dread the arrival of your regular monthly visitor, things get a little—shall we say—uneasy when Aunt Martha isn't her usual punctual self. And we all know that you wouldn't have anything to worry about unless, um, you had something to worry about.

So, rather than confessing to a slip-up that just might change your life forever, you could try a few of these explanations on for size—at least until the pee dries on your EPT stick.

➡ SOMETIMES THIS HAPPENS TO WOMEN WHO WORK OUT A LOT

In order for this to make sense, you would actually have to be a woman who works out a lot. And we're talking triathlons here, not the occasional Pilates class.

➡ SOMETIMES THIS HAPPENS WHEN YOU'RE UNDER A LOT OF STRESS

(Including the stress of possibly being knocked up.)

➡ I THINK I SKIPPED A PILL SOMEWHERE

It would have been an honest mistake, although it's kind of hard to mess up a daily medication with packaging straightforward enough that a chimpanzee could figure out the twenty-eight-day dosage. Let's all cross our fingers and say a little prayer to the Patron Saint of Ditzes.

➡ I THINK IT'S EARLY MENOPAUSE

If it is, get ready to experience a brave new world of hot flashes, night sweats, weepiness, and the occasional emotional tsunami. About the only good thing to come out of the reality of this excuse is that you can get so much mileage out of it as a pardon for any number of sins.

➡ I HAVE AN IRREGULAR CYCLE

Apparently, your better judgment is a little uneven as well.

ADDITIONAL EXCUSES FOR

MISSING
A PERIOD

➤ I'VE BEEN BANKING THEM.

➤ I WAS NEVER VERY GOOD WITH PUNCTUATION.

➤ THE GYM SHOWER SCENE IN "CARRIE" SCARRED ME FOR LIFE.

➤ I AM BOYCOTTING MENSES.

···EXCUSES FOR BEING···
THE MOM

The maternal instinct compels members of certain species to feed, nurture, and protect their young at all costs. Just as mama bears and she-gators will let you know in no uncertain terms when you have wandered a little too close to their brood, human mothers will go all Wild Kingdom on anyone who dares to put Baby in the corner. It's the natural order of things.

What we sometimes forget is that our young don't always appreciate the fierceness of motherhood—the instinct to wet tissues with our own spit for wiping off corners of mouths, to limit Internet time, to demand something more substantial than a Pop Tart for breakfast, to "lose" certain skimpy articles of clothing in the laundry, and to generally get all up in the business of our sons and daughters.

In those situations, you need to come up with not only a good excuse for your decisions but one that you can yell loudly over the din of a slamming bedroom door.

➧ SOMEDAY YOU'LL UNDERSTAND

Kids have no concept of the future or the slow, unfolding story line of life. "Someday" is about as tangible a thought as condominiums on the moon. So, when you pull this excuse out of your apron pocket, you are really using it as reassurance to yourself. You are planting a seed of hope that someday, when your child is an adult, there will be a moment of appreciation. Or, at least, pity.

➧ BECAUSE I'M YOUR MOTHER, THAT'S WHY

There is really no clever comeback to this point, which makes it a dependable (albeit lazy) conversation ender.

➧ AS LONG AS YOU ARE LIVING UNDER MY ROOF . . .

As keeper of the house, you call the shots. And you can go a long way with this reasoning if your child is of an age where he or she could actually move out. (The adult children you still have living in your basement are particularly vulnerable to this line of retaliation.) If tossing the kid out on his ear would bring on the wrath of Child Protective Services, however, then you might find this empty threat meeting resistance or dismissal and you having to resort to the old impotent standby of raising your voice and saying it louder.

➡ I DON'T WANT YOU TO END UP ON A MILK CARTON

Chase this one with a family viewing of *America's Most Wanted*. And remember that, in a plastic world, the life expectancy of this excuse is running out.

➡ CHILDREN CRAVE STRUCTURE

This one might work on the other soccer moms in the McDonald's drive-through, but not on the four-year-old whose cravings lean more toward opening the prize in his Happy Meal before (not) eating the cheeseburger.

➡ HOUSE RULES

Now if only enforcing them could be as easy as hanging them on the refrigerator.

➡ THIS IS HOW MY MOTHER DID IT

You can get away with this one if you are dipping candles or churning butter. All other instances are iffy. And make sure grandma isn't around to contradict you.

➡ THIS IS NOT HOW WE RAISED YOU

Assuming you are using this line in reaction to something your kid has done that would suggest that he or she was raised in a zoo or barn, then you need to either accept the fact that your child-rearing skills were not as sharp as you thought they were, or it's time to call the reform school.

➡ BECAUSE IT MAKES THE FAMILY LOOK BAD

Careful. Saying this is like handing your kid a trophy for being the black sheep of the family. And, although everybody wants to excel at something, this award is not coveted by many.

➡ YOUR LOSER FATHER MAY LET YOU GET AWAY WITH THIS, BUT I WON'T

It may feel good temporarily to take a dig at your ex while scolding the one-good-thing-you-did-together, but the aftereffects of this one aren't worth the momentary high.

➡ I HAD A BAD DAY AT THE OFFICE

If followed by an "I'm sorry," this could be your best move to cover just about anything short of felonies.

ADDITIONAL EXCUSES FOR
BEING THE MOM

➤➤ GARANIMALS ARE COMING BACK IN STYLE.

➤➤ SLUMBER PARTIES ALWAYS END IN A MASSACRE ANYWAY.

➤➤ YOUR MAMA!

➤➤ MY WORK HERE IS DONE.

➤➤ WHAT DO YOU MEAN I NEVER WRITE? DIDN'T YOU GET MY POSTCARD FROM VEGAS?

EXCUSES FOR PIGGING OUT

In moments of weakness, people have been known to satisfy their hunger cravings by a) ordering the biggest steak on the menu; b) treating themselves to a Dairy Queen trip; c) baking a pan of brownies with no intention of sharing; d) devouring a carton of cottage cheese and chasing it with a bag of Cheeto's; or e) all of the above.

The longer your caloric rap sheet, the more likely you will want to dip your ruffled potato chip into the bowl of creamy, ranch-flavored excuses that we've brought to this pitch-in.

➡ IT WAS ABOUT TO GO BAD

Mmmmmm! The only thing better than a little bit of salmonella is a whole lot of salmonella. And at least the Tupperware bowl of two-week-old chili won't go to waste. Or, at least it won't until it hits your system like a locomotive hitting a cow sometime around 2 a.m.

➡ I'M ON VACATION

Just because it arrives under a dome on a room service cart or adorned with a delicate orchid bloom doesn't make that fourth (or fifth or sixth) meal any less of a threat to your waistline. In fact, research has shown that food has the same caloric value in exotic time zones as it has in your own kitchen. Go fig.

Indulge with caution before your return flight, or you might be asked to check your oversized butt at the gate.

➡ I'M GOING TO THE GYM TONIGHT

Go ahead and tell yourself that. But you don't even want to know how many hours you would have to spend on the elliptical machine to counteract the crime you are about to commit in the Taco Bell drive-through.

➡ I'M STARTING MY DIET TOMORROW

Didn't you say that yesterday?

➤ I'M ANEMIC

Having a bona fide vitamin deficiency is like getting a free pass to eat something—fast! Not sure how much iron you're getting out of that entire sleeve of Oreos, though.

➤ IT'S A 100-CALORIE PACK

And 100 calories times 6 (the universally accepted serving size for these little teasers) equals 600 calories. Congratulations, you just ate a Big Mac.

➤ I DIDN'T WANT TO WASTE IT

Some people blame America's high obesity rates on over-processing and over-serving. We blame it on the endless childhood lectures about starving children in Africa.

Whether you're shoveling down the last ten bites of your farmhand breakfast, the untouched chicken fingers on your child's high chair tray, or the potato salad/nacho dip/ hot wing remains of your Super Bowl party after all of the guests have gone home, you probably aren't going to save the world with your resourcefulness.

➤ I ALREADY HAVE A BOYFRIEND/HUSBAND. WHY SHOULD I WORRY?

Maybe that's a question you should ask your boyfriend/husband's skinny new mistress.

➥ I DIDN'T EAT BREAKFAST

An extra serving of lasagna at lunch does not a bowl of cereal make.

➥ IT'S JUST A SNACK

As opposed to the meal-sized serving of Peanut M&M's?

➥ I NEED SOMETHING TO SOAK UP THE ALCOHOL

Since the damage has already been done (and the makers of Jagermeister would like to thank you for your continued support), you might as well add something of substance to the mix. And, of course, you will show a little more restraint with your choice of food than you did with your choice of beverage.

A nice, healthy salad sounds really good right about now, doesn't it?

➥ I NEED TO TAKE A PILL

To be fair, some medications advise against taking them on an empty stomach. It is safe to say, however, that nowhere in any medical journal will you find a study to back up your decision to lay a foundation of fried chicken before swallowing your cholesterol pill.

➥ IT'S MY METABOLISM

And your metabolism ordered the second stromboli?

ADDITIONAL EXCUSES FOR
PIGGING OUT

➤ I HAVE DECIDED TO TAKE UP COMPETITIVE EATING.

➤ THE AIRPLANE KEPT WANTING TO GO IN THE HANGAR.

➤ I'M GOING AS VEAL FOR HALLOWEEN.

➤ IT SAYS "ALL YOU CAN EAT," NOT "IF YOU CAN EAT."

·······EXCUSES FOR·······
SHOPPING

We live in a society that caters to the reptilian brain of credit card–wielding consumers. The temptations are out there, in every glossy magazine ad, high production-value Super Bowl commercial, and art-directed shop window. "Buy this. Own that. It will make your life complete." So, how could anyone blame you for going a little spastic with your plastic?

Well, it's all good, clean fun until somebody defaults on her Victoria's Secret card. When the nasty calls and letters from the collection agency start coming in, don't expect your Miracle Bra to work any miracles.

➡ IT WAS ON SALE

You don't have to be Suze Orman to figure out that spending nine dollars on something that regularly costs twelve dollars still puts you out nine dollars.

➡ I HAD A COUPON

News shows love to trot out those features on super-frugal families that scrimp and save and manage to get their hands on enough coupons to leave the grocery store with carts full of merchandise and purses just a few dollars lighter than they were when they walked in. Shame on them and their expanding folders—brimming with fifty-cent-off clippings from newspapers and cereal boxes—for leading us to believe that we too could live inside the world of *The Price is Right*.

The rest of us mere mortals play right into the hands of clever marketing, proudly throwing down a twenty-five-cent coupon on something that was already marked up fifty cents—just to justify all the time we spent clipping coupons out of the Sunday paper.

➡ IT WAS THE LAST ONE IN MY SIZE

This will be a tough sell if the article of clothing in question is a muumuu.

➡ IT WAS BOGO

Since when do two wrongs make a right?

➤ I NEEDED IT

There is a fine line between "need" and "want."

Scratch that. There is a big, fat, Magic Marker line between "need" and "want." Saying that you "need" designer fur-lined ankle boots to get you through the winter or the entire Ralph Lauren fall collection for your weekend in the country pushes the limits of necessity.

➤ I DON'T HAVE ONE IN THIS COLOR

Just because you dream in Technicolor doesn't mean you have to walk around in a matching wardrobe.

➤ I HAVE EARNED THIS

Maybe you have. Make sure you have also earned enough money to pay for it.

➤ IT WILL FIT AFTER I LOSE ALL MY WEIGHT

Sinister forces are at work in the universe. Why else would buying clothes a size or two down from what you are currently easing yourself into be such the kiss of death for any diet-and-exercise plan?

Keep this in mind, and don't be silly. Do you really want a closet full of size two's taunting you when your Weight Watchers plan runs amuck?

➡ IT'S RETURNABLE. I SAVED THE RECEIPT

If you are saying this, you have probably already looked at your car trunk full of shopping bags and felt a pang of buyer's remorse for having gotten a little carried away. You might have pulled out all of your purchases, lined them up on your bed, and attempted the painful Sophie's Choice of deciding which parts of your windfall will have to go back to the mall. It is a noble thought and one that might make you feel a little less out of control at the moment. But we all know that once something has made it home—once you have envisioned it as an accessory of your life—it's hard to set it free again.

➡ IT'S HELPING THE ECONOMY

And when you are invited to the White House to accept your medal of honor, you will have the perfect Chanel suit to wear.

ADDITIONAL EXCUSES FOR
SHOPPING

➤ MY MONEY TREE IS MOLTING.

➤ I'VE GOT TO KEEP REPLACING ALL OF MY CLOTHES THAT HAVE HOLES BURNED IN THEIR POCKETS.

➤ HOW ELSE AM I GOING TO MEET PEOPLE ... AND BY PEOPLE I MEAN SALESMEN WHO GET AN EMPLOYEE DISCOUNT AT NORDSTROM?

➤ I HAVEN'T DROPPED YET.

➤ THERE WAS A FREE GIFT WITH ANY $200 FRAGRANCE PURCHASE.

EXCUSES FOR SISTER RIVALRY

Just because she's the closest thing to you on the planet genetically doesn't mean that getting along has ever been easy. In fact, your proximity to her—both geographically and genetically—may well be a major contributing factor to your inability to deal with all of the bugaboos of a relationship you were born into. Thus, your need for so many excuses.

➡ SHE BORROWS MY CLOTHES ALL THE TIME

Often called into service when you need to justify why you have spirited away something from her personal collection of things, this excuse hits people where it counts. According to the universal rule of borrowing stuff, you are allowed one like exchange for everything that disappears from your stash and reappears in hers.

Be mindful of the articles in question, though. If you make off with the keys to her Miata, she has every right to track you down. Unfair as it might seem, she also has every right to do so while wearing your Lucky Brand jeans.

➡ I KNOW EXACTLY HOW SHE THINKS

Be thankful that you don't. If you knew what she was thinking at certain key moments in your lives, you'd probably never speak to her again.

➡ MOM/DAD ALWAYS FAVORED HER

Shouldn't that make you pissed at your parents, not her?

➡ I'M TIRED OF LIVING IN HER SHADOW

No matter how big a to-do people make about your sibling's accomplishments, it is not healthy to make your own mark by shredding her prom dress, writing "dork" on her locker, or heckling her during her campaign speech for class president.

Fast-forward a decade or two, and it is equally unacceptable (and just as pathetic) to trash-talk her at family reunions, wear Converse All-Stars to her formal wedding, or sell her Pulitzer on eBay.

➨ FIRST CHILDREN ARE ALWAYS SELFISH

True. Deal with it.

➨ MIDDLE CHILDREN ARE ALWAYS FREAKS

Even truer. Deal with it.

➨ THE BABY OF THE FAMILY IS ALWAYS A DRAMA QUEEN.

Truest of all. Deal with it. (And go ahead and enjoy the theatrics. It's great material for your memoir.)

ADDITIONAL EXCUSES FOR
SISTER RIVALRY

➤➤ I'VE ABANDONED HER FOR MY SORORITY LITTLE SIS.

➤➤ THE WOMB WENT DOWNHILL AFTER SHE MOVED IN.

➤➤ I HAVE DEVOTED MY LIFE TO GETTING BACK AT HER FOR SCORING THE PRETTIER CANOPY BED.

➤➤ THEY MADE A MOVIE ABOUT OUR RELATIONSHIP. MAYBE YOU'VE HEARD OF IT. IT'S CALLED "WHATEVER HAPPENED TO BABY JANE?"

➤➤ SHE DROPPED ME ON MY HEAD.

➤➤ I WANTED A BROTHER.

➤➤ PEOPLE ALWAYS SAID SHE WAS THE PRETTY ONE. UNTIL I SHAVED HER HEAD.

·······EXCUSES FOR·······
SMOKING

Have you heard that smoking is bad for you? Of course you have. You've been warned by everyone from the Surgeon General to your doctor to the wheezing old guy pulling the oxygen tank behind him at the state fair. But does that stop you from sneaking out on the back steps to puff one last cig before bedtime . . . or before the end of your break . . . or before it's time to pick up the kids at soccer practice? Not when you have so many so-called legitimate reasons to keep on lighting up.

➠ IT HELPS ME RELAX

You will have plenty of time to relax in the iron lung.

➠ IT HELPS ME THINK

Nicotine is a stimulant, you tell yourself as you rattle off the list of famously productive people with smoking habits. Still, it is likely that the only things you have in common with Albert Einstein, Thomas Edison, Winston Churchill, Oscar Wilde, Albert Camus, C.S. Lewis, Kurt Vonnegut, John Wayne, Miles Davis, and J.K. Rowling is a dry, unproductive cough and a collection of dirty ashtrays.

➠ IT'S THE ONLY TIME IN THE DAY THAT I HAVE TO MYSELF

Can't really argue with this one. Much like the porcupine's spiny armor and the skunk's musk, your own ring of secondhand smoke handily fends off intruders. In your natural habitat, it's just you, your smokes, and the ghoulish specter of lung disease.

➠ I ONLY DO IT WHEN I DRINK

Two charming habits rolled into one stumbling, slurring, tobacco-wreaking socialite! By the way, this reasoning makes sense to no one except your fellow bar smokers. Best-case scenario, you are preaching to the choir (which, incidentally, sounds a little like a Kim Carnes music video).

➡ I ONLY DO IT WHEN I'M AROUND PEOPLE WHO SMOKE

Peer pressure always yields a little bit of compassion. And grouping yourself in with a bunch of other people engaged in something equally offensive at least makes it hard for the offended to know where to direct their nasty sideways glares.

➡ IT'S MY BODY. IT'S MY BUSINESS

In saying this, you are also asking people to please disregard the secondhand smoke, ashes, and smashed butts that are the detritus of your habit.

Oh, by all means.

➡ IT MAKES ME FEEL SEXY

There was a time when movie starlets gazed half-lidded through swirling rings of smoke, and there was certainly something sexy about it. The sharp dialogue, sultry background music, soft lighting, and Vaseline on the camera lens that added a little va-va-va-voom are nowhere to be found when you are seen huddled and puffing away on the little designated smoker's bench outside your smoke-free office building.

ADDITIONAL EXCUSES FOR
SMOKING

➤ THEY WERE RIGHT IN JUNIOR HIGH SCHOOL.
IT IS ACTUALLY COOL.

➤ WASN'T IT BEN FRANKLIN OR ONE OF THOSE
OTHER FAMOUS QUOTE PEOPLE WHO SAID
"GIRLS THAT SMOKE ARE GIRLS THAT POKE?"
WHOEVER IT WAS, I'M JUST TRYING TO SEND A
MESSAGE THAT I'M INTO EASY SEX.

➤ TAR IS MY FAVORITE FLAVOR.

➤ I'VE COME A LONG WAY, BABY.

➤ YOU, DAD, I LEARNED IT FROM YOU.

EXCUSES FOR BAD

STUDY HABITS

Kids have it so easy these days, and not just because they have been spared the ten-mile walk to and from school in the snow. Instead of libraries and indexes, they have Google and Wikipedia. They can e-mail assignments and videoconference lectures. They can text and record from their cell phones. And there has been a significant uptick in the quality of coffee that is available for late-night cramming.

So why all the lame excuses for not showing up to class or for turning in your assignments late? Dog ate your homework? C'mon, you can do better than that.

➡ I'M NOT REALLY INTERESTED IN THE SUBJECT

Academia's equivalent to the "I'm just not that into you" approach does have some cred. It suggests that by not studying for the upcoming final on Gods and Empires in the Ancient Near East, you have made a conscious decision to screw up your GPA.

➡ I'M TRYING TO STRETCH MYSELF

You should be pretty limber after filling out your required hours with classes in yoga and Pilates this semester.

➡ THE PROFESSOR IS CREEPY

Could be. Particularly the creepy way he writes a D at the top of your half-baked term paper.

➡ COMPUTER CRASH

Tough to argue with this one. The first time.

➡ THE TEACHER DOESN'T TAKE ROLE

Hopefully, the teacher will show the same inattention to detail when grading the exam for which you were so woefully unprepared. Probably not, though.

➤ COLLEGE IS A TIME FOR EXPERIMENTING

You are away from home for the first time in your life, surrounded by other people who are away from home for the first time in their lives. The savages are running the island, and there are, shall we say, opportunities everywhere you turn.

Some experimentation is going to happen. That does not change the fact that at some point in your future—especially if you plan to run for political office or win a few Olympic gold medals—you will have to account for the wild times. This excuse will sound as hollow then as it does now, but it's really all you have to go with.

➤ WHY SHOULD I CONFORM TO WHAT ACADEMIA WANTS?

It's either that or conforming to what your shift manager at Burger King wants.

ADDITIONAL EXCUSES FOR BAD
STUDY HABITS

➤ IF I'M SUPPOSED TO BE A CO-ED, ISN'T THERE SUP-POSED TO BE SOMEONE ASSIGNED TO HELP ME?

➤ IT'S IN MY OTHER TRAPPER KEEPER.

➤ MY DOCTOR SAYS I'M ACANEMIC.

➤ ALL OF MY PENCILS ARE STUCK IN THE CEILING.

➤ I'M TOO COOL FOR SCHOOL.

➤ I AM D-LIGHTFUL!

EXCUSES FOR TATTOOS

The point might not be clear at the moment of bodily adornment (or even in the weeks or months leading up to your decision to get inked) that a tattoo is something that will stick with you forever. Longer than your favorite pair of jeans, longer than your toned triceps and firm lower back, and—you can almost bet on it—longer than the fella for whom you are about to permanently announce in big cursive letters your enduring love. You will wear this tattoo to your grandchild's graduation.

In the meantime, your fresh ink might give you the confidence you will need to pull off a very convincing reason for wearing your emotions on your sleeve. The following excuses get our tramp stamp of approval:

➡ OUR LOVE IS FOREVER

And hopefully the letters in his name can someday be altered into a large Celtic symbol. Just in case.

➡ EVERYBODY'S GOT ONE

Which makes a tattoo a great way to show the world your individuality!

➡ THEY LOOK COOL

Do we need to remind you that for about five minutes there, bell-bottom jeans looked really cool, too?

➡ IT'S IN A DISCREET SPOT

Then it will be a great conversation-starter during pelvic exams.

➡ IT'S ART

But unlike the painting over your fireplace, you can't change this one out when your taste in art matures or goes from, say, old-school nautical to the Arabic symbol for truth.

ADDITIONAL EXCUSES FOR
TATTOOS

➤ I SAW WHERE THE CIRCUS IS HIRING A NEW TATTOOED LADY.

➤ MY BELLY BUTTON WAS LONELY.

➤ IT'S ALL ABOUT BRANDING!

➤ I CALL IT A TITTOO.

➤ HOW ELSE AM I GOING TO REMEMBER THE SPELLING OF HIS NAME?

EXCUSES FOR
OFFICE DRAMA

You spend the better part of your week with the people who earn their paychecks beside you. Due to the sheer volume of time that you are in the company of each other, things are bound to get a little tense.

When the tension escalates into something regrettable (and, more than likely, entertaining for everyone who has gathered around to watch), you will need to do some spin-doctoring and damage control. These excuses might—or might not—renew your sense of job security:

➠ I AM TIRED OF COVERING FOR HIM/HER

A lot of people can relate to the lament of the over-burdened partner—the one who works through lunch while the other one is raising schooners of beer at the pub, the one who comes in an hour early to prep for a meeting that the other one walks into fifteen minutes late, the one who draws up elaborate memos and status reports that the other one simply initials.

For this reason, a lot of people will cut you some slack when you don't exactly bust your chops to finish his/her half of a project on time. But when you take that unscheduled two-week vacation in the middle of crunch time, you won't hear many atta girl's from the entire office that you leave hanging.

➠ IT'S NOT IN THE BUDGET

As heartless as it sounds, this is a perfectly viable excuse for almost anything that you don't want to take responsibility for obtaining. And hopefully you are not referring to toilet paper in the restrooms.

➠ THE MICROWAVE IS SUPPOSED TO BE FOR EVERYBODY

That doesn't mean it's okay to help yourself to whoever's bag of popcorn is in there.

➡ IT'S NOT MY FAULT THAT THE REPLY-ALL BUTTON IS SO CLOSE TO THE REPLY BUTTON

But it is your fault that you have now outed yourself with that office-wide "Well said, Pumpkin!!!" e-mail that you just sent out in response to the CFO's weekly update.

➡ I HAD NO IDEA THE BATHROOM WASN'T SOUNDPROOF

That excuse doesn't fly when it refers to both diarrhea and diarrhea of the mouth.

ADDITIONAL EXCUSES FOR

OFFICE DRAMA

➤ I DRINK A LOT OF WATER. SO, OF COURSE I SPEND A LOT OF TIME AT THE WATER COOLER.

➤ NEPOTISM SOUNDS SO PRETTY WHEN YOU SAY IT.

➤ WHEN I SAID THE BOSS SUCKS, I MEANT BRUCE SPRINGSTEEN.

EXCUSES FOR PURSE MALFUNCTION

Often, they enter our lives as fashion statements—sleek, attractive accessories plucked from the rack based on their potential to look cute with the shoes and outfits already in our clothing arsenals.

With time, they become something more utilitarian. Practically extensions of our bodies. And when they cause problems in our lives (or when they really aren't causing problems in our lives but serve as an easy scapegoat), they deserve their own special set of excuses.

➡ MY PURSE DUMPED

This works well as a catch-all for general dishevelment.

➡ I CHANGED PURSES THIS MORNING

You can sell this to your girlfriends when you can't come up with that coupon for the free entrée at Applebee's you've been squirreling away. You will have a harder time getting the officer to buy it as the reason why you can't locate your driver's license and registration.

➡ MY PHONE WAS BURIED IN MY PURSE

Buried even deeper was your desire to take the call.

➡ MY KID MUST HAVE PUT THAT IN THERE

It could be as innocent as a crumpled Snickers bar wrapper or as incriminating as a Nine Inch Nails CD. If an embarrassing item tumbles from your purse when you pull out your makeup bag, you can always try blaming it on sabotage. People might not buy your story, but it will help you deal with the humiliation.

ADDITIONAL EXCUSES FOR
PURSE
MALFUNCTION

➤ **I WAS A MARSUPIAL IN A PAST LIFE.**

➤ **I AM A MAGICIAN, AND THIS IS HOW I PRACTICE THE PULLING-A-RABBIT-OUT-OF-A-HAT TRICK.**

➤ **IT'S A BLACK HOLE.**

➤ **I DON'T CONTROL THE PURSE STRINGS.**

THE ULTIMATE EXCUSE:

It is the ultimate Get Out of Jail Free card. The ultimate conversation ender. The ultimate reason for biting the heads off of the ones you love. The ultimate excuse for nearly any sin a woman can commit.

When we sat down to write this book, we could not think of a single situation in which those three letters could not be applied. Which is why we decided to give them their very own section. What better way to pay tribute to a condition that has, in its own twisted way, contributed so much to the women's cause?

Because the world has resolved to tuck its tail between its legs and accept PMS as a universal truth, its applications are far-reaching. Fellow women will commiserate with the mood swings, cramping, body aches, need for chocolate, and unwillingness to get out of bed or use a hairbrush. They will come to your defense, often with ginger tea and heating pads. Men will simply bow to the mystery of it all, like primitives at the mouth of a volcano.

This, Dear Reader, is power. Use it.

part 2

REAL AND IMAGINARY GREAT WOMEN'S EXCUSES

It is common knowledge that, throughout history and in the realm of literature and fable, men have made excuses for their behavior. From "I am not my brother's keeper" through "I did not sleep with that woman," some have even become household phrases.

Are men just more likely to make excuses for their behavior than women? Probably.

On the other hand, there is the distinct possibility that women would have made just as many excuses—if they had been given the chance. The secondary role women have been forced to take in much of world history and literature prior to the 20th century naturally limits the number of famous, quotable excuses they've uttered in efforts to extract themselves from awkward situations.

But far be it for us to let facts get in the way of some cheap laughs. Herein you will find our speculated excuses for famous real and imagined women of the past . . . and a few from the present.

To set the tone, we begin with the woman who might or might not—depending on what you believe—have started it all.

➡ EXCUSES FOR EVE

Let us now consider Eve, the first lady of the Bible. Eve, as the story goes, had everything she needed in the Garden of Eden but couldn't resist the temptation to dine on the fruit of the tree of knowledge. Result: She and Adam were shown the door. Or the gate. Or whatever it was that they couldn't return through. (Other side effects might include pain in childbirth.)

What's an independent, one-of-her-kind woman supposed to say when called out for disobeying the big guy in the sky? She could have tried these:

→ I thought it was a plum.
→ Something must have been lost in translation. I don't speak serpent very well.
→ Adam told me to.
→ The sun … the one you created on the fourth day … was in my eyes.
→ Forbidden fruit? I thought you said 'forbidden lute.' And I'm not big on music anyway, so I figured, you know, easy to honor that rule.
→ I was just going to make fritters. Surely there's nothing sinful about fritters.
→ You're the one who put questions in me, Mr. Almighty.

➡ EXCUSES FOR GREAT WOMEN OF FICTION

Now let's speculate on possible excuses for imaginary women—those created by playwrights, screenwriters, and whatever it is you call people who create fairy tales. Not storytellers. What's the word we're looking for?

Oh, never mind.

➡ EXCUSES FOR JOCASTA

Bad enough she had to abandon her son, Oedipus, far from Thebes after an oracle pronounced that the kid would kill his father and marry his mother.

But things got worse when the grown-up kid heard the same prophecy and decided to skip his adopted home and head back to, you guessed it, Thebes.

And there, well, you probably already know what happened.

So, as much as Mama—and everyone else—were victims of fate, the situation had to still be socially awkward. So, excuses were no doubt needed. Sophocles, the playwright, didn't fill those in. We will.

→ I thought he looked familiar.
→ It's complex, Oedipus.
→ You never know who you're going to meet at a toga party.
→ They're all Greek to me.
→ Son of a . . .

➥ EXCUSES FOR JULIET

Not only did Shakespeare's most famous heroine need excuses to cover up the fact that she was hooking up with the son of a rival family, but she also had to put off Paris, the guy picked out for her. (Think Chino in West Side Story, if it's been a while since you read the CliffsNotes.)

Had she lived, she would also have some explaining to do about accepting drugs from Friar Lawrence. Here, we help a sister out:

→ Never was there a guy of so much Woooah! as this Romeo.
→ Who can you trust if you can't trust the clergy?
→ You wonder why there was confusion? Who can understand any of this Shakespeare talk?
→ He reminded me of Tony, this guy I met on the west side.
→ The apothecary made me do it.

➡ EXCUSES FOR MADAME BOVARY

She's a doc's wife who breaks her matrimonial vows, spends like crazy, and otherwise makes a mess out of her life and the lives of those around her. She's Emma Bovary, and the novel about her by Gustav Flaubert is considered one of the best ever. Certainly the best book ever written in which the title character kills herself with arsenic, her husband preserves her room like a shrine, and their daughter ends up working in a mill.

So what excuses does this French woman have to divert attention from her questionable behavior? Knowing the answer to that would require us to actually read the book. Which we both keep saying we'll do, eventually.

In the meantime, here are some excuses for Madame Bovary that we don't expect to encounter in the book's pages. But wouldn't it be cool if we did?

→ I couldn't Flaubert it anymore.
→ Just like Belle sang in *Beauty and the Beast*, I want much more than this provincial life.
→ I was only a doctor's wife, but I sure could operate.
→ Well, excuse moi!
→ I Bovery acted. (Note: This is Lou's favorite excuse in the whole book. That says something both about Lou and about this book.)

➡ EXCUSES FOR CINDERELLA

She was a mistreated gal who only wanted to go to a royal ball. Against her: two wicked stepsisters and an evil Queen. On her side: a fairy godmother and, depending on which version you are citing, a bunch of mice. Result: a nice night on the town, a missing glass slipper, a visit from the Prince, and some happily-ever-after.
Were excuses in order? Perhaps.

→ You try dancing backwards in glass slippers.
→ I'm a clock-watcher. Can't help it.
→ Two words: Step. Sisters.
→ My other gown had mice hair on it.

➡ EXCUSES FOR THE OLD WOMAN WHO LIVED IN A SHOE

And you think the Octomom is bad. This woman had a nonspecific number of children and had no idea what to do. We're pretty sure if one of her neighbors was a reality show producer, he would know exactly what to do.

No doubt, she needed some excuses.

→ I'm Catholic.
→ I couldn't afford a big enough minivan.
→ I like to amortize my clothing purchases.
→ It's all Dr. Scholl's fault, the bastard.
→ Lifetime Channel, take me away.

➡ EXCUSES FOR RAPUNZEL

She was a long-haired prisoner who lowered her hair first to let her captor/parental figure witch climb up, then to do the same for a handsome prince. Eventually, she escaped but, we suspect, had to come up with some excuses both before and after.

→ I was just having a bad hair month.
→ Hair today, gone tomorrow.
→ That's not a hair in your soup it's … a wheel of dental floss.
→ My split ends wound up in three different counties.
→ Everything I know about relationships I learned from my witch captor.

➡ EXCUSES FOR SLEEPING BEAUTY

She pricked her finger. She dozed. She dozed some more and she dozed some more. Then she dozed. And kept dozing. Until eventually she was awakened by a handsome prince.

Sleeping Beauty, explain yourself:

→ I had a big turkey dinner.
→ I took a little too much Nyquil.
→ I didn't realize it wasn't the non-drowsy.
→ I was having a really nice dream.
→ I forgot to set my alarm.
→ If you didn't want me to sleep, you should have put a pea under my mattress.

➤ EXCUSES FOR SNOW WHITE

She almost got axed by a huntsman. She met up with seven industrious little people. She took a bite of the wrong apple (thanks, Magic Mirror), and she lay comatose until yet another prince made the rounds and woke her up.

Snow White's turn to weasel out of situations:

→ I like short men.
→ Green apples rock.
→ Someday my prince will … you know what, I'm not going to go there.
→ My stepmother's mirror told me to.

➤ EXCUSES FOR LADY CHATTERLEY

Her lover gets the title of the book, but it's Constance who sparks the action in D. H. Lawrence's then-sizzling 1928 novel by cheating on her paralyzed husband. The result led to obscenity trials and a not very good movie.

So what excuses might Lady Chatterley have tried?

→ When my husband told me he was impotent, I thought he said "important."
→ What can I tell you? The lady is a tramp.
→ He was a gameskeeper and I wanted to see if he was, you know, game. Nudge, nudge, wink, wink. Know what I mean?
→ I'm hoping that if they ever make a movie about my life, they will cast Pia Zadora as me.

➡ EXCUSES FOR MRS. VOORHEES

Her cooking for the kids at Camp Crystal Lake may not have been particularly noteworthy, but (SPOILER ALERT!) when she started hacking apart teens—paying special attention to those who reminded her of the counselors who allowed her son to allegedly drown—well, that's hard to ignore.

She's the true villain of the original *Friday the 13th* movie. And she surely could have used some excuses—not just for her own actions but for her (SPOILER ALERT!) still alive and deadly kid.

→ Most kids could use a nice summer at camp.
→ I thought hockey would keep him off the streets.
→ The children just didn't appreciate my gorp.
→ The s'more, the s'mearier.

⇒ EXCUSES FOR THE WOMEN OF "SEX AND THE CITY"

Samantha was a self-professed "try-sexual" who put cougars on the map. Charlotte had fidelity issues. Miranda once ate cake out of a trash can. And Carrie "couldn't help but wonder" how she would be able to spin her girlfriends' latest sexual exploits (oh gee, thanks) into material for her sex column.

None of the foursome (or their scriptwriters) seemed too concerned about making excuses for their behavior. But when VH1 gets around to making its *Sins and the City* tell-all, we've come up with a few for them:

→ Sometimes Big isn't big enough.
→ My sex swing gave me a cramp.
→ Pour me.
→ The wardrobe department made me do it.
→ I don't know what the Sam Jones you are talking about.
→ I was trying to give the camera my best angle, and I'm pretty flexible, so there you have it.

➡ EXCUSES FOR THE WICKED WITCH OF THE WEST

L. Frank Baum made her an evil ruler. A later novelist and Broadway musical made her a heroine. What they agree on is that the Wicked Witch aggravated Dorothy, the little girl from Kansas, who eventually doused her with H_2O.

Hey Witch, you got something to say?

→ I can't help it. I love shoes.

→ You try governing over munchkins.

→ The damn Potter kid took all the good brooms.

→ When life gives you monkeys, you can at least make them fly.

→ I had an allergic reaction to a new moisturizer.

→ I was bitter after once again being denied membership in the Lollypop Guild.

→ Nobody liked me at boarding school except for my roommate, who didn't like me at first, then she did. But she kind of turned on me when I stood up for all of the animals in Oz and . . .

part 3
EXCUSES FOR GREAT WOMEN IN HISTORY

Now let's get on with the big names in history, from the notorious to the saintly, from biblical times to present day.

All of these excuses are, as we said, speculative. So don't go trying to find them in history books. (Although, just for laughs, you can try to add them to their corresponding Wikipedia entries.)

➡ EXCUSES FOR DELILAH

Before we go into the excuses for Delilah, let's brush up on her story. It seems that she was given the task of figuring out the source of Samson's strength. So she asked. And he lied. So she asked again. And he lied. Guess what happened the next time she asked? Yep. He lied again.

On the fourth query, though, he answered, telling her that he and God had this little agreement about never cutting his hair. So, while Samson was sleeping, Delilah ordered his seven locks of hair to be clipped off. Then she turned him over to the Philistines, who . . . Well, why go into it? Let's just say it wasn't pretty.

What was Delilah's excuse? The Bible doesn't tell us. But we can speculate.

→ He needed a haircut anyway.
→ I just can't say no to a Philistine.
→ I thought our relationship was based on honesty. And he lied to me three times.
→ If I stay in my place, Tom Jones will never sing a song about me.
→ Do you know how hard it is for a woman to get a head in this world?

➤ EXCUSES FOR JEZEBEL

Here's another biblical person best known for the implications of her name rather than what she actually did. Here's what we know:

Jezebel was a Phoenician princess who married King Ahab and led him away from the Hebrew god and toward Baal. This, according to the Bible, included sexual immorality and ordering the death of Yahweh's prophets.

She continued pulling strings after her husband died, as her two sons took turns in power. Eventually, she was tossed out a window and left to be devoured by dogs. (This, after putting on makeup and inspiring the phrase "painted Jezebel.")

So what could her excuses have been?

→ I was just an early multi-culturalist.
→ This country just doesn't understand Baal-sy women.
→ Guess that old time religion isn't good enough for some people.
→ The Holy Books were short on memorable women. I did what I could.

➥ EXCUSES FOR SALOME

In most cases, excuses should never have to be made for dancing. In the case of Salome, well, an exception to that rule should be made.

To review: Herod was having a birthday. Salome was asked to dance as part of the evening's entertainment. Afterwards, the big guy gave what is probably the highest rating ever given to a dancer: He told her that whatever she asked, he would do (up to but not to exceed half of his kingdom, if we're reading the Gospel of Mark correctly).

Salome asked her mother what she should request. Mom, who clearly had issues, told her to ask for the head of John the Baptist.

She did. And although the king wasn't crazy about the idea, he was even less crazy about breaking his vow. So the executioner was called. Soon the head was in Salome's hands. She turned it over to bloody Mama. And the rest is infamy. (Plus a play by Oscar Wilde and an opera by Richard Strauss.)

Here are some possible responses if Salome were asked, "What's your excuse?"

→ Doesn't it say earlier in the Bible that we should honor our mother?

→ I was referring to John the Baptist as the whole John the Baptist movement. And so when I said "the head of John the Baptist," I meant the guy in charge. I just wanted to meet him. Seemed charismatic and interesting.

→ Just taking a walk on the Wilde side. Get it? Oscar Wilde? Wrote a play about me?

→ My feet hurt. It happens to dancers. Give me a break.

➡ EXCUSES FOR MARY

We know full well that when you are the widely accepted mother of the messiah, you don't need excuses. Still, it's fun to speculate.

→ God did it. Deal with it, Joe.
→ I'm allergic to frankincense.
→ He was a nice boy who just fell in with the wrong crowd.
→ You try living with a son who thinks he's perfect.
→ Carpenter, my foot. My door has been squeaking since Passover.

➡ EXCUSES FOR CLEOPATRA

She hooked up with Caesar. And after he was assassinated, she hooked up with Marc Anthony, one of the conspirators. She even hooked up with her brothers.

Egypt's most famous B.C. female politician/royal, Cleopatra eventually killed herself by snakebite. The 1963 film version of her life, starring Elizabeth Taylor, just about destroyed the 20th Century Fox film studio.

A no-excuses sort of woman? Yes. But if she weren't, here are some she might have tried:

→ I thought I'd mix it up a little and cease him.
→ It was all part of a pyramid scheme.
→ If you're going to have incest, it's best to keep it in the family.
→ I'm a sucker for a guy in a toga.
→ 'e gyped me. (More amusing if said with a silly Eliza Doolittle accent. But, then again, almost everything is more amusing when said with a silly Eliza Doolittle accent, right gov'ner?)

➡ EXCUSES FOR JOAN OF ARC

Most nineteen-year-olds have graduated high school and are wondering what college party to attend.

By the age of nineteen, however, Joan of Arc had led the French army. She had also, unfortunately, been captured, turned over to the Brits, and burned at the stake.

→ Who doesn't like steak?

→ God told me to. And sometimes, I wish he would have just told me to, I don't know, just go to Nineveh or something.

→ I misunderstood the term French fried.

➡ EXCUSES FOR LUCREZIA BORGIA

There's a good chance that 16th-century Italian noblewoman Lucrezia Borgia—wife of Giovanni Sforza, Alfonso of Aragon, and Alfonso d'Este—doesn't deserve her reputation as a backstabbing, poisoning (via a secret compartment in a ring), manipulative so-and-so. But since history has branded her a backstabbing, poisoning (via a secret compartment in her ring), manipulative so-and-so, we thought we'd give her some excuses.

→ My dad is the Pope, I can do what I want.

→ Donizetti's opera would be pretty dull if I wasn't so colorful.

→ I got frustrated trying to pronounce Sforzas.

→ I had to put something in my hollow ring. Were you expecting Kool-Aid?

➡ EXCUSES FOR LADY GODIVA

Legend has it that she famously rode nude on horseback through the streets of Coventry because … bet you don't remember why, do you? Didn't think so. But don't feel bad, we didn't either until we looked it up.

Turns out her hubby had imposed some serious taxation on them. She tried to get him to rescind the taxes and he wouldn't. Until her requests finally led him to pull an "alright, alright … but only if … ."

That "if" was the unusual request that she take the famous ride. She did, with the understanding that by decree, all windows would be shut. The one guy who did peek earned a name even more famous than Lady Godiva's . . . Peeping Tom.

We'll leave his excuses for another book. For our purposes, Lady Godiva might have had some of her own.

→ Taxation without breast representation isn't fair.
→ I thought you literally meant bare back riding.
→ I was high from too much chocolate . . . maybe they should name a brand of that after me.
→ The horse needed to take a walk, and I didn't have a thing to wear.
→ Don't try to saddle me with your outdated morality.

➥ EXCUSES FOR BETSY ROSS

There's no evidence to support the story that she sewed the first U.S. flag. Still, she's such a part of American mythology that attention should be paid.

And excuses should be offered.

→ I dig guys in uniform.

→ Sew?

→ I read that horizontal stripes are slenderizing. Or did I get that wrong?

→ Stars go with my bonnet.

→ I just wanted to meet Thomas Jefferson. He's dreamy.

➡ EXCUSES FOR MARIE-ANTOINETTE

She was Queen of France, and legend paints her as being far from the Queen of Tact. The story goes that, when told that the people of France had no bread to eat, she said, "Qu'ils mangent de la brioche," which tends to be translated as "Let them eat cake." How rude.

Of course, there's no evidence that she actually said this. Even if she did, there was certainly plenty of brioche to go around. Whether she said it or meant it, the French revolutionaries were not impressed. They led her to the guillotine in 1793.

What might have been her excuses—should she have needed them?

→ I was just trying to get ahead. Get it. A head? Merde, guillotine jokes never go over very well during a revolution. And, yes, I know Salome already tried this one.

→ What I said was, "Qu'ils mangent de la brooch." It was a dare. A joke. I didn't think anyone would actually try to eat my brooch.

→ Who doesn't like cake, anyway?

→ I was trying out a different kind of powder that day, if you know what I mean.

→ I was feeling les miserables.

→ I was having a big hair day.

➥ EXCUSES FOR FLORENCE NIGHTINGALE

"The Lady of the Lamp," as she was nicknamed, became a legend for her pioneering work in nursing. What that has to do with lamps, we're not quite sure. But we know that she has a reputation just shy of Mother Theresa when it comes to not needing excuses.

We thought we'd give her some anyway.

→ I was sick of guys hooting, "Hello, nurse!"
→ So I like starched fashions, big deal.
→ Sensible shoes rock!
→ I got booked to sing in Berkeley Square and was in a hurry.

➡ EXCUSES FOR ROSIE THE RIVETER

She symbolized the spunk and the get-the-job-done spirit of home front women during World War II. She—and the very real women she fictionally represented—also made clear that women were just as capable of doing the work of men.

There was a real Rosie, by the way. That was Rose Will Monroe, who worked for a munitions factory in Michigan that supplied bombers to the Air Force.

What excuses could she have used?

→ I was riveted.
→ I was too busy doing the work of five men.
→ Sorry I was five minutes late. Silly me. I was doing the housework, feeding the kids, getting them off to school, taking care of my husband's parents, weeding the garden, and paying bills. Can I start my ten-hour shift now?

➡ EXCUSES FOR HELEN KELLER

Oh, come on. Did you really think we were going to sink so low as to offer excuses for the famed blind/deaf woman who went on to become an accomplished writer, speaker, and subject of junior high jokes?

Do you really think we would, for instance, list such excuses as "I lost it in the sun," or "Sorry, I didn't hear you?"

Of course we wouldn't. So just move along. Nothing to see hear.

➡ EXCUSES FOR LIZZIE BORDEN

Allegedly, she took an ax and gave her mother 40 whacks. When, so the rhyme goes, she saw what she had done, she gave her father 41.

Well, recent scholarship indicates that Lizzie Borden may, in fact, be innocent. But as was said in *The Man Who Shot Liberty Valence* (a movie that perhaps seven women have actually seen), "When the legend becomes fact, print the legend."

So we're going to with that. We're going to work with the assumption that Lizzie did, in fact, wield the ax.

So what could have been her excuse?

→ My parents wouldn't give me enough anytime minutes. Would have been nice to have unlimited texting, too.

→ It was the Axe Effect.

→ Axe me again, I didn't hear the question.

→ Who axed you?

→ You know how annoying it is when your mother tells you to do something right away and then adds, "Chop, chop!" at the end of the sentence? I really, really hate that.

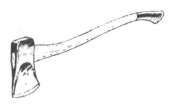

➥ EXCUSES FOR EVA PERON

She was the first lady of Argentina. And she had a huge, almost cult-like following. But none of that would matter to pop culture history if it weren't for the fact that the *Jesus Christ Superstar* guys, Tim Rice and Andrew Lloyd Webber, decided to write a musical about her and scored an unlikely hit that likely is being revived this weekend at a theater near you. (Don't bother with the Madonna film version, though, unless you want to swoon over a very hot Antonio Banderas—which is never a bad thing to do if you find yourself with a little extra time.)

What was Evita's excuse?

→ Don't ask me for excuses, Argentina.
→ Dictator, Schmictator.
→ If sexual indiscretions are good enough for most members of British Parliament, why shouldn't they be good enough for a major South American country?
→ I knew what I Juan-ted.

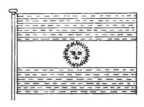

➠ EXCUSES FOR BONNIE PARKER

She made up one-half of America's most notorious outlaw couple, robbing gas stations and banks, killing police officers, and eventually, being ambushed and killed in Louisiana. Years later, as portrayed by Faye Dunaway, she spawned not just a hit movie but also a fashion frenzy.

Bonnie, what do you have to say for yourself?

→ It was the Depression. I was depressed.
→ Have you seen gas prices lately?
→ If Clyde looked more like Warren Beattie, maybe we would have found other things to do.
→ He had a gun in his pocket and he was happy to see me.

➠ EXCUSES FOR TYPHOID MARY

More than fifty people are said to have been infected by this cook, who was ordered to get out of the food prep business but returned anyway. Her name is now synonymous with the spreading of disease. In her case, it was typhoid fever.

History doesn't record her excuses. So we made some up.

→ It's nice to share.
→ Anti-bacterial lotion was still far away in the future.
→ Disease-ridden hands, warm heart.
→ You think I'm bad, you should see my sister Typhoon Mary.
→ And if you think me and Typhoon Mary are bad, you should see our cousin Typo Maryy.
→ Or my nephew MikeTyson.

⇒ EXCUSES FOR TOKYO ROSE

The notorious broadcaster of Japanese propaganda during World War II wasn't just one person. The moniker was slapped on about a dozen women attempting to influence the morale of U.S. soldiers.

What could her (their) excuses have been?

→ Every rose has its thorn.
→ Hell, it's show business.
→ Something got lost in translation.
→ Bad sushi.

⇒ EXCUSES FOR AMELIA EARHART

She was the first woman to fly the Atlantic and quickly became the world's most famous aviatrix. Alas, her final flight didn't go so well. During her attempt to circumnavigate the globe in 1937, Earhart's plane went down just short of Howland Island in the Pacific Ocean—due to either miscommunication, equipment failure, or simple operator error.

And darned if that last part isn't what people tend to remember most about one of history's most trailblazing women. If she'd had a chance, here are some of the reasons she might given for, um, flying off the handle.

→ I lost me in the sun.
→ I needed to get rid of some excess baggage.
→ I didn't put my tray table in the upright position.
→ My husband gave me directions.
→ The media hog Lindberg needed to be taken down a peg or two.
→ Stupid security checkpoint.

➤ EXCUSES FOR JUDY GARLAND

She went over the rainbow, hung out with Andy Hardy, starred in *A Star is Born* and then, well, things got a little messy.

But through four divorces, big problems with taxes, drug dependency, and far too many bad female impersonators trying to do her act, she remained—and remains—a one-of-a-kind performer.

Excuses for Judy? Sing it.

→ Everything I learned about marriage I learned from Mickey Rooney.

→ Lies. All lies. Or maybe I mean, Liza. All Liza.

→ Tight ruby slippers.

→ A star was bored.

→ I asked someone how I get to Carnegie Hall and instead of just saying "Practice," he said, "Let others define your self-image, screw yourself up, and then maybe practice."

➡ EXCUSES FOR JOAN CRAWFORD

To a generation, she was one of Hollywood's leading actresses, winning a Best Actress Oscar for her performance in *Mildred Pierce* and a cult following for such camp classics as *Whatever Happened to Baby Jane*.

For many, though, the image of Crawford that comes to mind is less from her films and more from her estranged daughter's tell-all bio *Mommie Dearest*, which painted her as emotionally and physically abusive. The film version of the book, starring Faye Dunaway in all of Crawford's penciled-in-eyebrows and padded-shoulder glory only solidified that image.

→ She must have confused me with Bette Davis. Everyone does.
→ Wire hangers just don't hold the shape of the garment the way wooden ones do.
→ You'd be pissed, too, if you went from Grand Hotel to appearing opposite a guy in a caveman suit in *Trog*.
→ Surely you have me mistaken for Broderick Crawford.

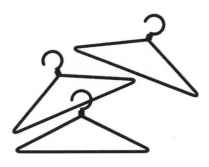

➤ EXCUSES FOR ELIZABETH TAYLOR

As a young actress, Elizabeth Taylor captivated the world with performances in such films as *National Velvet*, *Lassie Come Home*, and the original *Father of the Bride*. She grew into a major star, with *Cat on a Hot Tin Roof* and *Giant*, but she hit the wall with *Cleopatra*, the bomb for which she broke the $1 million-a-film ceiling.

Credits since then were rockier. For the past few decades, though, she's been better known for her jewelry, her charity work, her defense of pal Michael Jackson, and her eight husbands.

What excuses become a star most?

➔ Screw Marilyn Monroe, diamonds are my best friend.
➔ Mickey Rooney and I got drunk one night and made a most-marriages bet.
➔ I was afraid of Virginia Woolf.
➔ I was Queen of Denial.

➡ EXCUSES FOR MARILYN MONROE

Indelibly etched in the history of Hollywood, thanks to such classic films as *Some Like It Hot*, *The Seven Year Itch* and *Gentlemen Prefer Blondes*, Marilyn Monroe is one of a handful of performers whose image is known worldwide. As fascinating to follow off screen as on, she survived famed marriages to diametrically opposed men—playwright Arthur Miller and baseball great Joe DiMaggio.

Notoriously difficult on set, the woman no doubt had better excuses for herself than the ones we came up with.

→ I don't know. Something just got up my skirt.
→ If I'd known Elton John would scrap my lyrics for Princess Diana, I wouldn't have done any of it.
→ A nation turned its lonely eyes away from me. Ew, Ew, Ew.
→ The marriage just seemed like one big crucible.
→ Percodan is a girl's best friend.

➡ EXCUSES FOR ROSA PARKS

Bus boycott legend Rosa Parks didn't need any excuses and we're not going to pretend to come up with some for her.

Go, Rosa!

➡ EXCUSES FOR CHER

Cherilyn Sarkisan has been part of a chart-topping pop duo, an Academy Award–winning actress, a solo star, an icon for gay men (in the rarified company of Marilyn, Judy, and Bette), an infomercial entrepreneur, and an oh-my-god-what-is-she-wearing fashion eyebrow-raiser. Through it all, she's been herself—even as she seems to have turned into plastic woman.

Here, we "cher" some of her possible excuses.

→ I was born in the wagon of a travelling show. That ain't easy, with the bumps and all that.
→ Our love won't pay the rent.
→ It's all men, brother.
→ I was moonstruck.
→ I enjoyed being in *Mask* so much I figured I'd look like I'm wearing one permanently.

➡ EXCUSES FOR OPRAH WINFREY

At the risk of her never, ever, ever picking this humble book as one of her club selections, we now speculate on some excuses the queen of talk television and the nation's tastemaker might make.

→ A Steadman is hard to find.
→ Dr. Phil owed me a lot of favors. Still does. A lot.
→ I read it in a book somewhere.
→ Maya Angelou told me to.
→ Excuse? Well . . . here, have a car. Do I still need an excuse?
→ If my house looks a little messy right now, it's only because Tom Cruise just left.

➡ EXCUSES FOR MADONNA

We don't need to fill you in on the life and career of Madonna. And we don't need to tell you that she's definitely a no-excuses kind of woman. But if she were someone who would make excuses for her behavior, here are some possibilities:

→ You got a problem with me releasing a seemingly endless book of nude photos of myself?
→ You got a problem with movies that suck (except for *Desperately Seeking Susan*, of course)?
→ You got a problem with crappy children's books?
→ You got a problem with my attempt to circumnavigate adoption laws because I'm me?
→ Bite me.

➡ EXCUSES FOR TONYA HARDING

She coulda been a skating legend and trailer park hero. Instead, she got involved—or her ex-husband Jeff Gillooly got involved—or something, we really couldn't follow—in a brutal plan to kneecap her competition, Nancy Kerrigan, at the 1994 U.S. Figure Skating Championships.

That would have been enough. But then a sex tape she had made with that very same ex-husband began making the rounds. She then was booked on a domestic violence charge for punching her boyfriend (a different guy, this time). Then she boxed—and beat—alleged Bill Clinton gal pal Paula Jones.

Need we go on? This woman was a walking excuses handbook.

Here are some purely imaginary possibilities:

→ I knee-ded to do it.
→ I needed a video of my honeymoon because I was too toasted to remember it.
→ I've always been a connoisseur of the sweet science of boxing. Susan Sontag and I often got together for brunch to discuss its nuances.
→ I just liked saying "Gillooly." You're saying it right now, aren't you? "Gillooly. Gillooly. Gillooly."
→ I thought Nancy Kerrigan had stolen my chewing tobacco pouch.

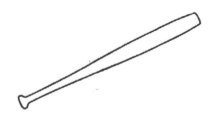

➤ EXCUSES FOR LINDSAY LOHAN, PARIS HILTON, ET AL.

Our hope is that this book has a shelf life longer than just a few weeks. So we're going to dispense with too many biographical details or retelling of particularly sordid incidents involving Lohan, Hilton, etc. because the turnover rate for tabloidable names is pretty fast. By the time you pick this up, there could well be a whole new crop of why-exactly-are-they-famous? party girls keeping themselves in the headlines with their eyebrow-raising antics.

No matter who the latest train wreck may be, though, these excuses could well apply to any of them:

→ My other car has my panties in them.
→ I'm with even stupider.
→ It's either this or work.
→ The paparazzi. It's their fault. You know, the ones who show up where my publicist tells them I'll be and have the nerve to take my picture.
→ I was paid an appearance fee. So I appeared to be an ass.
→ I'm doing it for the economy. Without my BS, lots of newspaper and TV people would be out of work.

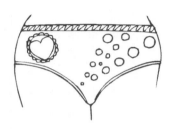

➡ EXCUSES FOR HILLARY RODHAM CLINTON

She took center stage during her husband's Presidential stint first by attempting to lead the health care reform charge and then by standing by her man during a series of sex scandals. More recently, she took a serious run at the White House and ended up with a major consolation prize—secretary of state.

Here are a few excuses for her to file away with the divorce papers:

→ Woke up. It was a Chelsea morning. And I went back to sleep.
→ When I told her to put it on my bill, I didn't mean it that way.
→ It was part of the vast right wing conspiracy.
→ My hands were tied by the U.N.
→ Barack's orders.
→ Spare the Rodham, spoil the child.
→ It's Ahmaginedad's fault.
→ It takes a Village Pantry.

➡ INDEX OF EXCUSES

[Insert accomplished person's name here] did it, too   19

After what he did to me . . .   82

Ageism.   48

As long as you are living under my roof . . .   122

Because I'm your mother, that's why.   122

Because it makes the family look bad.   124

Children crave structure.   123

College is a time for experimenting.   148

Computer crash.   147

Einstein had a cluttered house.   32

Even the Amish are allowed to go nuts once.   88

Everybody's got one.   152

First children are always selfish.   140

He really does still love me, no matter what he said.   83

He was an artist.   66

He was really hot in high school.   36

He's a diamond in the rough.   37

He's going through a rough time in his marriage.   41

He's going through a separation.   41

He's lucky I didn't do worse.   82

His wife has put on a lot of weight.   43

His wife is going to screw him over in the divorce anyway.   41

His wife is ruining his life./He deserves better.   83

House rules.   123

I already have a boyfriend/husband. Why should I worry?   129

I always go for the bad boy.   37

I am a product of my environment.   19

I am tired of covering for him/her.   155

I barely have time to breathe, let alone read.   53
I can't do bangs.   24
I changed purses this morning.   160
I couldn't get a babysitter.   110
I couldn't get the kids moving this morning.   109
I couldn't relate to the characters.   53
I didn't eat breakfast.   130
I didn't have a sober buddy.   87
I didn't have a thing to wear.   109
I didn't know he had a girlfriend/wife.   37
I didn't like the selection.   53
I didn't mean to send it.   102
I didn't want to dirty up the kitchen.   76
I didn't want to ruin my nails.   114
I didn't want to waste it.   129
I don't do it all the time.   18
I don't have one in this color.   135
I don't kiss ass.   49
I don't know what they like.   106
I don't want you to end up on a milk carton.   123
I guess I wasn't the right "Man" for the job.   48
I had a bad day at the office.   124
I had a coupon.   134
I had a husband and kids to worry about.   71
I had a little too much to drink.   36
I had no idea the bathroom wasn't sound-proof.   156
I had to stop for pads.   109
I hate wearing the same thing every day.   96
I have a headache.   114
I have an irregular cycle.   118

I have bad lighting at home.   97

I have earned this.   135

I have such fine hair.   24

I have to get up early tomorrow.   110

I have to wash my hair.   110

I just need some time off.   60

I just wanted it out of my eyes.   25

I just wanted to make sure you were okay.   91

I know how exactly how she thinks.   139

I like where I am right now.   49

I lost my loyalty card.   77

I need something to soak up the alcohol.   130

I need to take a pill.   130

I needed it.   135

I needed the benefits.   71

I needed to de-stress.   88

I needed to eat.   71

I never really had any talent.   71

I only do it when I drink.   18, 143

I only do it when I'm around people who smoke.   144

I only see them once a year.   106

I paid a lot of money for this.   97

I raised my own children. I don't have to raise yours.   105

I ran out of Swiffers.   30

I saw it on the red carpet.   96

I saw you with that other girl.   61

I skimmed it.   54

I still had the key.   82

I think I skipped a pill somewhere.   118

I think it's early menopause.   118

I think we're better as friends.   59

I thought I left something at your house.   91

I told my hairdresser I wanted to try something different.   25

I tried some new product.   23

I wanted to be fashionably late.   110

I was drinking tequila.   87

I was drunk.   66

I was in a rut.   96

I was in the neighborhood.   91

I was just trying to help.   102

I was out of eggs.   76

I was out of flour.   77

I was waiting for the cable guy.   110

I was young.   66

I went to bed with wet hair.   23

I work all day.   113

I'm an adult.   18

I'm anemic.   129

I'm between hairdressers.   25

I'm defrosting next week.   32

I'm going to the gym tonight.   128

I'm growing it out.   23

I'm in the process of decluttering.   32

I'm just here to get out of the house.   54

I'm not really interested in the subject.   147

I'm not very athletic.   113

I'm not your maid.   30

I'm not your mother.   31

I'm on vacation.   128

I'm parting it differently.   24

I'm starting my diet tomorrow.   128

I'm tired of living in her shadow.   139

I'm trying to quit.   19

I'm trying to stretch myself.   147

I've just been feeling so disconnected lately, and I don't know why.   58

I've met somebody else.   61

It has sentimental value.   31

It helps me relax.   143

It helps me think.   143

It looked cute on Renee Zellweger.   25

It looked really cute in *Lucky* Magazine.   96

It makes me feel sexy.   144

It shrunk in the wash.   98

It slipped.   102

It was a school night.   110

It was about to go bad.   128

It was BOGO.   134

It was good enough for us.   106

It was no big deal anyway.   103

It was on sale.   134

It was the last one in my size.   134

It wasn't see-through when I put it on this morning.   97

It will fit after I lose all my weight.   135

It works in the movies.   83

It's a 100-calorie pack.   129

It's a designer label.   98

It's a free country.   91

It's a marriage in name only.   43

It's a new perm.   25

It's art.   152

It's doing the dishes that gets to me.   77

It's helping the economy.   136

It's in a discreet spot.   152

It's just a snack.   130

It's laundry day.   97

It's my body. It's my business.   144

It's my metabolism.   130

It's not in the budget.   155

It's not like I'm proud of this.   19

It's not my fault I knew all of his passwords.   82

It's not my fault that the Reply All button is so close to the Reply button.   156

It's not my weekend to clean.   30

It's not you, it's me.   59

It's returnable. I saved the receipt.   136

It's so hard to get kids to do their chores.   31

It's something I started in college.   18

It's the only time in the day that I have to myself.   143

It's what's best for the kids.   59

Middle children are always freaks.   140

Mom/Dad always favored her.   139

My boss is an idiot.   48

My cleaning woman quit.   31

My college didn't really prepare me.   72

My electricity went out this morning.   24

My GPS screwed up.   91

My husband/boyfriend didn't put the keys back where they were supposed to be.   109

My kid missed the bus.   109

My kid must have put that in there.   160

My phone was buried in my purse.   160

My purse dumped.   160

My shoes were killing me.   87

Nothing else fits me anymore.   97

Only nerds tuck in their shirts.   98

Our love is forever.   152

People were going to find out anyway.   102

Please don't judge me.   19

She borrows my clothes all the time.   139

Since when is that illegal?   36

Somebody had a camera phone.   66

Someday you'll understand.   122

Someday, years from now, when I'm not nearly this hot, I'll be happy
     that I preserved an image of me when I had it all together.   67

Sometimes this happens to women who work out a lot.   118

Sometimes this happens when you're under a lot of stress.   118

Sorry, I didn't hear you.   106

Supermarkets annoy me.   76

That was supposed to just be for us.   66

That's what I get for being too good at my current position.   49

That's what you're supposed to do at a bachelorette party.   87

The baby of the family is always a drama queen.   140

The box said it was temporary color.   26

The microwave is supposed to be for everybody.   155

The pill makes me gain weight.   113

The professor is creepy.   147

The tattoo is meant to remember the good times and/or so I don't make
     the same mistake again.   83

The teacher doesn't take role.   147

The two-state-distance rule.   42

There was nothing in the fridge.   76

They look cool.   152

This is how my mother did it.   123

This is not how we raised you.   123

This is what's best for both of us.   58

This town really isn't so bad.   72

Those dirty dishes aren't going anywhere.   30

We had a power failure.   77

We reconnected on Facebook.   36

We were off the clock.   88

We're consenting adults.   41

We're two different people.   61

What she doesn't know won't hurt her.   42

Why should I conform to what academia wants?   148

With a coupon, it's cheaper to eat out.   76

You are too good for me.   58

You only go to spring break once. Okay, maybe twice.   88

You weren't picking up the phone.   91

You're just not my type.   60

You're the only person who knows.   18

Your loser father may let you get away with this, but I won't.   124

➨ ABOUT THE AUTHORS

JULIA SPALDING is an editor at *Indianapolis Monthly*. She co-authored *The Encyclopedia of Guilty Pleasures* and plays on a roller derby team under the alias Valerie Hurtinelli.

LOU HARRY is also the author or co-author of *The Underground Manual of Office Dares*, *The High-Impact Infidelity Diet: A Novel*, *Creative Block*, *Kid Culture* and a stack of other books. By day (and sometimes night), he's arts and entertainment editor of the *Indianapolis Business Journal*. He knows he should have some explanation for being the wrong gender to co-write a book such as this, but frankly, he's all out of excuses.

Either author, barring any last-minute excuses, would enjoy speaking to your book group. You can reach them at workforlou@aol.com.

➨ ABOUT CIDER MILL PRESS

Good ideas ripen with time. From seed to harvest, Cider Mill Press brings fine reading, information, and entertainment together between the covers of its creatively crafted books. Our Cider Mill bears fruit twice a year, publishing a new crop of titles each Spring and Fall.

Visit us on the web at www.cidermillpress.com
or write to us at 12 Port Farm Road
Kennebunkport, Maine 04046